lady in the red dress

lady
in the
red dress

by david yee

Playwrights Canada Press
Toronto

Playwrights Canada Press
202-269 Richmond St. W.
Toronto, ON M5V 1X1
416.703.0013 • info@playwrightscanada.com • www.playwrightscanada.com

We acknowledge the financial support of the Canada Council for the Arts, the Ontario
Arts Council (OAC), the Ontario Media Development Corporation, and the Government
of Canada for our publishing activities.

Cover design by Leon Aureus
Book design by Blake Sproule

LIBRARY AND ARCHIVES CANADA CATALOGUING IN PUBLICATION
Yee, David, 1977-
Lady in the red dress / David Yee.

A play.
ISBN 978-0-88754-907-6

I. Title.

PS8647.E44L34 2010   C812'.6   C2010-902252-1

Fourth printing: September 2017
Printed and bound in Canada by Imprimerie Gauvin, Gatineau

MIX
Paper from
responsible sources
FSC® C100212
www.fsc.org

This play is dedicated to the 81,000 Chinese who paid the Head Tax, to the countless number who were kept from their families and loved ones during the Exclusion, to those who died building the foundation of this country only to be disavowed and forgotten.

Foreword

Given the position David Yee occupies in the nation's independent theatre food chain (and in the criminal imaginary), I suspect there may be some readers who will be surprised, to say the least, to find me penning this foreword. I would like, therefore, to clarify from the outset that my participation here has nothing to do with the recent legal dispute in which David Yee and I were, rather sensationally, involved.[1] I would also like to make clear that while this foreword counts towards hours of community service required for a previous peccadillo, I will receive no other favours or benefits, financial, commercial or otherwise, for writing it, as would normally be the case with celebrity preambles.

***

I'm not, it's true, exactly *objective*. I did some dramaturgical duty on this script. When Yee first asked me if I would serve as a dramaturg for his new play, I was reluctant. I told him I was trying to go clean, break free from the indie theatre and its attendant, darkly seductive lifestyle. My immigration "consultancy" was taking off and I felt this was maybe my last chance to start over, but Yee was insistent. He reminded me of the promises we'd made growing up together back in the 'hood, promises to "keep it real 4 ever." I, in turn, reminded Yee that we hadn't grown up together in the "'hood." I was the privileged child of Argentinean equestrian aristocracy, while he, admittedly, had grown up an opportunity-deficient child in one

---

1   The so-called "expired medication scandal." Those who followed the case closely will recall that I was more or less completely exonerated. Accounts in the so-called mainstream press lacked the necessary context and relied far too much on Western medical "experts" to give a full and accurate account of the situation. For a more nuanced explanation, see my article "Too Old? When Western Notions of Time Conflict with Efforts to Make Medications Available to People Far Away." *The Alberta Journal of Alternative Commerce*, Vol. 22.

of Mississauga's differently advantaged neighbourhoods.[2] Shaken, Yee muttered, "You've changed. It used to be about the music."

So, I asked him to tell me about his project: *Lady's Red Dress*. He did. I thought it was a mistake and told him so. I said, "Writing a play based on a song is almost always a bad idea. There's a reason it's a song. And in this case," I said, "the song is pretty slim. I mean, 'Spanish Train,' okay. That might make an interesting play. Or a graphic novel even. But 'Lady in Red,' it's thin." Yee looked shocked. "This is how I roll, dramaturgically, dog. I calls 'em as I sees 'em. If we're going to work together, I will speak the truth," I warned him. "That song," I continued, "I find it mawkish, uxorious even." Yee denied his play had anything to do with any Chris de Burgh song whatsoever, but my finely honed dramaturgical nose, trained to spectrographic sensitivity over hundreds of developmental workshops in poorly appointed facilities, knew he was bluffing. "I just don't see it sustaining for an entire play, and I don't think it's right for your brand." Of course, time and the fu-GEN production have only proven me wrong. Yee managed to find a whole lot more in that tune than I ever imagined possible. The whole *Chinese* angle, for example... I just had no idea. But that's what an artist does. Finds stuff that wasn't there and makes it be there.

I am, in fact, surprised by the amount of stuff Yee made be in his play.

It looks, at first, like it's a play about the redress campaign waged by Chinese Canadians in response to Canada's shameful Head Tax and Exclusion Act. Yee covers many of the details of this campaign, its backstory, the complications and legalities, so I won't discuss them here—not that I actually know the particulars anyway. But the issue of redress, it seems to me, is really only a pretext for the play. The feds, after all, offered a (not legally binding) apology in 2006, expressed the government's "deepest sorrow for the subsequent exclusion of Chinese immigrants," and offered "symbolic payments" of $20,000 "to [approximately 400] living Head Tax payers and living spouses of deceased payers,"[3] much as described in the script. What's up then?

While redress may be a done deal legally and politically, it's far from over *psychically*. In terms of an individual's or a community's psychic life, a legal settlement of this kind marks the beginning rather than the end of a process

---

2 Yee doesn't like to talk too much about those days—perhaps the memories are too dark— but he did once tell me, "I wasn't unaware of the rougher elements in the vicinage." His use of the litotes is, I think, telling. (Though he has long since left the violence of the suburbs behind, the traces are still visible. Even today, years later, Yee smokes and often swears.)

3 Prime Minister's Office webpage. http://www.pm.gc.ca/eng/media.asp?category=2&id=1220. While some claimed no desire for redress payments, many felt this settlement didn't go far enough.

towards justice, healing and reconciliation. There is much to work through before the long-term effects of such a history can be left behind.[4] Yee materializes the unseen but powerful psycho-emotional currents that no legal decision can contain or subdue in Sylvia, the lady in the red dress herself. She, as Max, with tremendous psychological perspicacity, notes, has "anger issues." Quick with the quips, out of a film noir I can't quite name, or a *bande dessinée* I never read: performing, deforming and ultimately destroying the China-doll trope, jumping o'er time with her knife-throwing and throat-slitting routine, Sylvia is vengeance herself. If the government's apology is the state's performance of affect (in its expression of sorrow, for example), Yee's *Red Dress* could be considered a theatrical victim-impact statement.

Still, the play isn't only a revenge fantasy, a working-through of the potent and destructive emotions engendered by a long history of racial (and in Sylvia's case, sexual) oppression and discrimination. No, there's more here.

Like, what's up with the poetry? I'm not saying it doesn't make a kind of sense. Sure, some classy lines about anarchy and an impending bloodbath seem apposite in Sylvia's mouth, but we wonder—I do anyway—where, when, why did Sylvia—and Danny—learn Yeats?[5] Yeats? Symbolist, aristocrat, mystic and *IRISH*? What's that *doing* in a play "about" the Exclusion Act/Humiliation Day/Head Tax Brouhaha?

What about the Brothers Chan, Happy and Biff, with their urban idiolects? They have an obvious narrative function as keepers and performers of an intermedial (as the PhDs like to say) collective and historical memory that Max must learn, experience and, even, to some extent, embody. But their language, the way they speak, points away from that over-determined history and towards possibilities for self-definition and invention that figures such as Tommy Jade and even Sylvia do not enjoy.

The Chans, that olde Irish Poet, as well as Yee's sly references to theatre and performance seem to me—and again, I'm just a disbarred barrister doing some consulting—to be making trouble. These unexpected, conflicting, at times complementary, languages challenge the monologism of racist discourse and disturb the tidy racial boundaries in which some of the powerful characters in the play deeply invest.[6] *Red Dress Lady* is a play about historical

---

4   Like Jin says, in a line unfortunately neither eloquent nor rhythmical, "Each time they harass me I wanna explode / We should ride the train for free, we built the railroads." "Learn Chinese" from the album *The Rest is History*. Ruff Ryders/Virgin Records, 2004. For Real.

5   I know they didn't actually learn it. I know: they're characters in a play.

6   Plenty of real folk were invested in these boundaries too. That's what the whole Exclusion Act was about, wasn't it? "They [the Chinese] will never assimilate with the Anglo-Saxon race, nor is it desirable that they should." The Honourable Mr. Justice Crease, judge of the Supreme Court of British Columbia. 1885 Royal Commission. Many years later, some folks continue to

wrongs and a perhaps flawed reparation effort, but it situates that narrative within a theatrical present that simultaneously recognizes and rejects the categories invoked by that history. The play, in the profusion of voices and the several time frames it embraces, stages and celebrates heterogeneity. Its central figures are, after all, two mongrels, two half-breeds: Sylvia, the always-already mixed past our nation emerges out of, and Max's son, Danny, the otherworldly, "twice-blessed" future we just might be able to make our way towards.

There's more, but making that be there is up to you, reader, actor, director and producer. My work here is done. Once again I feel beneath my heels the ribs of Rocinante. I fought the law and the law won. Got to keep on keeping on.

Guillermo Verdecchia
Aruba, 2010

---

invest in, and defend, these boundaries.

Preface

In our morale must lie our strength:
So, that we may behold at length
Routed Apollo's
Battalions melt away like fog.
—W.H. Auden

lady in the red dress began as a response to an email I received from an MP in British Columbia. The email itself was in reply to a petition I had signed in opposition to Bill C333, which attempted to quietly sweep a number of issues (including the Head Tax and Exclusion Act) under a decidedly cheap rug. The MP's email accused the CCNC (who initiated the petition) of being liars and media whores with no real basis for complaint. It was libellous at best. My response was a vitriolic rant of some five pages in length. I didn't send it, precluding the satisfaction of Some Secretary's finger hitting the delete button. Instead, I took his sentiments and used them to create the foundation of a character. And that's how I came to meet Max Lochran.

Things change, of course. Writers write, dramaturges dramaturge, actors act. When that oversimplified process is all said and done, you're left with (hopefully) a richer world with characters who are more than vilified cardboard cut-outs of politicians you hate. And sometimes they are exactly that, but it is by design and not default.

In 2006 I was subcontracted by the Canadian government to design the media presentation that would play before Harper's parliamentary apology was broadcast in Toronto. When they asked who to make the cheque out to, I said "Irony." Okay, I made that part up, but the rest of it is true. If you attended the Toronto viewing of that address, those images of sad, broken Chinese migrants were my doing. It was to my understanding they wanted a "happy collage" representing the Chinese experience in Canada. What they actually got were close-ups of images sourced from old photographs of the 1907 anti-Asian riots in Vancouver. Small rebellion.

Like Tyler Durden splicing frames from xxx films into *Bambi*, I felt my subversive misappropriation of the redress event was inappreciable. The insubstantial reparation efforts and consequent historical whitewashing was still underway. We paid the *danegeld*, got some of it back, and we're still not rid of the motherfucker (my apologies to Kipling).

And that's when *lady in the red dress* underwent a paradigm shift. It became the voice of unrest and dissent, and the enemy of repentance. I took issue with the language of the apology. I took further issue with the conditions of the redress. The self-satisfied, ingratiating and disingenuous humility on display just added further ignominy. Yes, it's an angry-sounding play, sure, and people will dismiss it at that. But I don't actually consider *lady in the red dress* to be an "angry play" or a "vengeance play." I prefer to think of it as a play that refuses to forget. It (loudly) considers the effect this shit has really had on all of us Asian Canadians. Or just Canadians.

Because I don't *really* believe you need to heal to move forward. I do believe very strongly that you need to look where the fuck you're going. The Auden epigraph, with the *morale* and *melted Battalions*—it might mean different things to different people, but to me it means that the good fight is a long one. The apology and redress, the subjects of this play, are only the beginning. The road ahead is still the road ahead. And the fight is still worth winning.

David Yee
Ibiza, 2010

lady in the red dress was developed under the auspices of Factory Theatre's CrossCurrents Festival, Playwright Theatre Centre's Playwrights Colony, Diaspora Dialogues and fu-GEN Theatre Company, and with the support of the Toronto Arts Council through their Playwrights Program. The play premiered at the Young Centre for the Performing Arts, Toronto, on January 24, 2009, with the following company:

Stewart Arnott	Coogan, Hatch, Doctor, Stryker and John
Ins Choi	Tommy Jade, Willy, Biff and Happy
Nicco Lorenzo Garcia	Danny
Laura Miyata	Sylvia and Mirabel
Richard Zeppieri	Max

Directed by Nina Lee Aquino
Assistant direction by Karen Ancheta
Set and props design by Camellia Koo
Lighting design by Michelle Ramsay
Costume design by Jackie Chau
Composition, sound design and musical direction by Romeo Candido
Sound design assistance by Kevin Centeno
Stage managed by Kat Chin
Apprentice stage management by Neha Ross
Fight consultant & Cantonese coaching by Richard Lee
Choreography by Clare Preuss

Characters

Biff Chan
Daniel Coogan
Danny Lochran
Doctor
Happy Chan
Thomas Hatch
John Lochran
Max Lochran
Mirabel Coogan
Lt. Stryker
Sylvia
Tommy Jade
Willy Chan
Secretary

Zero: Sylvia vs. The Failure

1964. A living room in a suburban home. Tables and lamps are knocked over, one light flickers on and off, pitching us in and out of darkness. JOHN *Lochran is on the floor in that room, he is a bloody mess. He speaks to another figure. In the inconsistent darkness we see only glimpses of her form... flashes of her red dress.*

JOHN   I'm sorry, okay? There wasn't anything there. I looked, I kicked over every stone there was and there's nothing there. I swear to Christ. I tried. I did everything you asked me to!

Beat. JOHN *looks for some reaction from his captor but gets none. His breathing is laboured. He tries to get to his feet but falls back down onto his knees.*

He doesn't exist. It's not even a real name! Like you made it up... sounds made up... *(beat)* You can't expect me to tell one from the other.

Movement. The red dress is pulled up slightly to uncover a knife strapped to the leg it reveals. The knife is unsheathed and twirled expertly between the fingers that hold it, the blade catching the light as it continues to flicker.

JOHN *tries to back away but crumples under his own weight.*

There is no Tommy Jade! I looked—goddammit—I *looked*! There's no trace of him, not anywhere...

He falls flat onto the floor, the fight has nearly gone out of him. He looks up pathetically at the knife-wielding lady.

I don't believe in you! Just a story that... my father told me: Oriental—goes completely off the reservation... starts killing white people. He was all... magical, he'd float in and out of rooms, quote—poetry—or something, then slashed their throats. And he couldn't die. *(beat)* But that was just something fathers told their sons so they'd be careful of you people. Just a story...

Beat. The lady in the red dress starts towards JOHN, slowly... stalking him.

That was twenty years ago... and you're just a girl. You're just a girl. And there's no such thing as that thing... this is the world... not the story... it can't be real... you can't be... you're just a girl...

She gets closer to him.

Please... I have a family... I have a son! I have a—so you take *him*, okay? You take—like a trade, okay? You can have my son... you take him... and you let me live, okay? *(Beat. He calls for his son.)* Max! Max, come here...

Quickly, the lady grabs JOHN by his throat and lifts him up to meet her eyes. She stares into him, cocking her head. Curious. This feels somehow different. She throws him down. He begs her.

Blood is blood, right? Doesn't matter. Shouldn't matter. Right?

She is upon him again. She grabs him by the hair and pulls him to his knees.

Please! I'll do anything you want! Please... *(Pause. She silently stares at him.)* Jesus Christ, just say *something*!

Beat.

SYLVIA   "Mere anarchy is loosed upon the world,

The blood-dimmed tide is loosed, and everywhere
The ceremony of innocence is drowned."[1]

> *She wrenches his head around, exposing his neck to her, and slits his throat ear to ear. Then unceremoniously drops the body to the ground. An afterthought, she reaches into the dead man's shirt pocket and retrieves a packet of cigarettes. She removes one, lights it, and throws the pack back on the floor. She starts to leave, but stops near a family photo in a small frame. She picks it up and stares at it.*

Max.

> *She breaks the glass of the frame and removes the photo. She leaves the room, a trail of smoke behind her.*

One: Max vs. The World

2006. The Department of Justice. Downtown Toronto. Early morning. MAX Lochran is on his Bluetooth headset.

MAX   What we're *proposing*, Linda, is a formal "statement" and a settlement in the amount of x dollars to each of the individuals who paid the Head Tax. If they're still alive. *(beat)* The statement? Well, it's a statement, I don't know... *(beat)* Apology? *(nervous laugh)* We would *prefer* the term "acknowledgement" just to clear up any—what is that—*inference* around liability. But very respectful. Very... remorseful. Something like: We respect blah blah blah and acknowledge blah blah blah, we welcome Chinese yadda yadda and this won't happen again zippidy do da day. Sound good? *(beat)* What? No, only the *individual* who paid the tax. Or a spouse, but they'll need proof. No one else, no *families*. *(beat)* We've been over this. Linda, we have—Christ.

The liability to the rest of—to all of them—we can't sustain that. The class action filed against the federal government in 2002, if you *remember*, Linda, didn't hold legal water because we proved conclusive juristic reason, meaning you did NOT prove substantial enrichment to the government. If we, you know, start going crazy and saying that we owe everyone, Linda, *everyone*... that

---

1   "The Second Coming," W.B. Yeats.

this was a real *thing* that—we'd be fuck soup. *(beat)* I don't know. Soup made of… fuck, I guess—it's just a saying, it's what the kids are saying. *(beat)*

No. No. No, goddammit—look, this is a reasonable offer, Linda. Moreover, it's a *realistic* offer. Even above that, Linda, it's an *offer*. Period. We don't *have* to do anything here. The lawsuit was knocked out of court and your bargaining power went with it. This settlement—reparation—whatever… it's a good deal. *(beat)* Linda, hold on, I've got another—what is that—hold on—

He switches calls.

Max Lochran. *(beat)* What?! *No*, don't send him… I can't—this is—he shouldn't…

DANNY, MAX's teenage son, a high-functioning autistic, walks into his office.

Dammit. Danny, what are you doing here, you should be in school. This is—we have *talked* about this, you can't just—

DANNY hands him a note. MAX reads it quickly.

Take your kid to work day? The fuck is that? Sorry, Danny, I didn't mean to say—fuck—this is not a good…

DANNY begins to sulk. MAX quickly switches gears.

Hey, you know what? Today, Danny, *today*… you are gonna be my special helper, okay? How does that sound? Pretty great, huh? So, you can… uh… *OH*!

He walks DANNY to the door.

You know how I'm always coming home late and you're always whining—or, *expressing*… how you feel about that? Well, it's because I keep getting lost in this *big* office… so how about you go with Secretary…

He yells out the door.

SECRETARY!

Back to DANNY.

...and you make me a special treasure map of the entire—
Danny—the *entire* office. So I don't get lost anymore? Okay? *(beat)*
There she is now, so why don't you... and Danny, don't call her—
try not to call her—a "cunt" again, okay? That's... that's Daddy's
special name for her that he uses at home. Okay? There you go.

He all but shoves DANNY *through the door. Without skipping a beat,
he touches a button on his headset, transferring to the call he had
on hold.*

Linda. Look, we are giving $20,000 to each of the poor bastards
that paid the tax. *(beat)* Around eight million in total. Yah, pretty
big number, pretty *generous* number. I mean, let's not get carried
away here, they paid $500 each. What is that, that's a nothing
number in the grand scheme of... yes, we considered inflation,
that's *why* we are paying out— *(beat)* Hold on, I got another—

He switches calls.

Max Lochran. *(beat)* Hatch, great, I needed to—can we reschedule? I've got a hundred and fifty things today, and this bitch from
the CCNC on the other—yah, she's on hold, can I—thanks.

He switches calls.

Altogether? What is "altogether"? What they paid? Back then, all
of them? *(beat)* Twenty-three million. *(beat)* Equivalence today?
Look, those numbers fluctuate all the time, it's one amount, then
another, depends on market values for one and what programs
the funds went into, long-term/short-term... what that would
be in today's currency is a bit more difficult than... *(beat)* 3.6
billion? *(He laughs loudly, then stops.)* Yah, that's what we got too.
(shifting gears) But it's not a numbers game, Linda, you have to
understand that...

DANNY walks into MAX's office with a huge roll of drafting paper.

Dammit. Hold on—

He places her on hold.

Danny! I *told* you the *entire*—

DANNY unrolls the paper to reveal an exquisitely detailed blueprint of the office.

That... that is actually remarkably detailed...

DANNY   Take elevator two. Elevator two is even and prime. Elevator two is thirteen feet closer to your parking spot than any other elevator.

MAX   Elevator two...

DANNY   *(indicating the path he has drawn for MAX)* Follow the yellow line and you won't get lost again.

MAX   What's that red line?

DANNY   The red line is the path you should never take. If you find yourself on the red line, you should stop and immediately go back to the yellow line.

Follow the yellow line, Max.

Beat

MAX   That's good, Danny, you— *(He tries to touch his son's head but can't quite make himself do it.)* You're a good... *(He gives up.)* Is it to scale?

DANNY just stares at him.

Is it to scale, Danny?

DANNY shakes his head.

Then it's not perfect, is it? So why don't you... just... you're just going to have to do it again. Okay? You want it to be perfect, right? So you should...

He waves him out the door. He dials his secretary.

Secretary. You know who came up with "take your kid to work day"? Fucking *teachers*. Apparently it's not enough to only work five months outta the year, they need *one more day* to pawn off *their* responsibilities on *us*. *(beat)* I just don't have time for this today. Not today. Keep him busy. *(beat)* And get Starling on line two. *(beat)* And *no more calls about the Chinese thing*.

He tries to switch calls, but his left arm won't move. He pinches it a couple of times, then switches calls with his right hand.

It's a lesser amount because we can't compensate people who aren't around anymore. Some of those guys don't have their papers, some of them are dead, I mean... we're a coupl'a generations away from this whole thing even being *relevant*, y'know? *(beat)* No, I'm not *saying* that, I'm *illustrating*—look, Linda, twenty grand is a good offer. You're not going to get any more, but it's entirely possible that if you keep up this endless—yes, *endless*—bargaining... it's possible you will get *less*. I don't want that any more than you do, okay? I'm on your side here. *(beat)* Well, yah, I'm on their side, too... but I'm a *negotiator*, Linda, that's what I *do*—

He switches calls and gets out a bottle of bourbon from his desk. He unscrews the top with his one good hand and takes big swigs during the next exchange.

Max Lochran. *(beat)* Judge Starling, great. I'm afraid I have to reschedule our review meeting. *(beat)* I think I'm having some sort of heart attack. *(beat)* It could be a stroke, I don't know. It could be—what is that—palsy, can you just *get* palsy? I'll call you tomorrow, have Secretary schedule something.

He switches calls.

Linda. *(beat)* Quote me? No you can't quote me, you cannot commit to paper the words that have come out of my mouth. When I *say* something, you can quote it. You don't quote this conversation, Linda, because I am just *fucking* ILLUSTRATING.

He ends the call. He tries to breathe. Beat. He passes out.

Two: Max vs. Sylvia

MAX wakes up face down on his desk in his office. The bottle of bourbon has spilled and turned sticky. SYLVIA walks in the door.

SYLVIA   Max.

MAX   What...?

SYLVIA   Are you all right, Mr. Lochran?

MAX   What? I'm... yes, I'm fine. Everything is— *(He tries to lift his left arm, it works perfectly.)* Hm... how can I, uh?

SYLVIA   Is something wrong?

MAX   Bad dream, I guess. I thought I was having... but I suppose I was mistaken.

SYLVIA   Drinking so early, I imagine you'd be mistaken about a lot of things.

MAX notices the bottle.

MAX   Shit.

He starts mopping it up with random papers and things.

Sorry, I'm not usually—that is to say, I don't usually—

SYLVIA   And what are you... usually? *(She sits herself down and lights a cigarette.)*

MAX   Usually I'm a guy who wouldn't let you smoke in his office.

SYLVIA   And today?

MAX   Today I'm going to join you. *(He checks his pockets.)* I don't... I forgot, I guess, could I—

> *SYLVIA takes a long draw, then seductively slides her cigarette between his lips. She leaves it there and stands. He draws and holds it.*

SYLVIA   So this is your office...

MAX   It is.

SYLVIA   Your chair.

MAX   My chair, my desk, my... I was going to label it all, but I thought that might be... ostentatious. Or something.

SYLVIA   You're taller than I imagined.

MAX   I drink a lot of milk. What exactly do you want?

> *Beat.*

SYLVIA   Have you ever looked into the eyes of a killer?

MAX   A few.

SYLVIA   They're different. Aren't they? Eyes, normal people's eyes... you look into them and you see who they really are.

MAX   What is this?

SYLVIA   But killers, the eyes of a killer... they're reflecting pools. You look into the eyes of a killer and you see yourself. Every dark, murderous thing you keep hidden. Every thought you're not allowed to have. What we're capable of, Mr. Lochran. In the eyes of killers we see what we're capable of.

Beat.

MAX   Sure.

SYLVIA   What do you see when you look in *my* eyes, Mr. Lochran?

     MAX looks her in the eye. Beat. He is lost for a moment. Disoriented.
     Spellbound.

     "The unfinished man and his pain
     Brought face to face with his own clumsiness;
     The finished man among his enemies?—
     How in the name of Heaven can he escape
     That defiling and disfigured shape…?"[2]

MAX   "The mirror of malicious eyes
     Casts upon his eyes until at last
     He thinks that shape must be…" something something—what
     is that? Yeats, isn't it? "A Dialogue of Self and Soul," or…
     something.

SYLVIA   *(She smiles at this.)* That's right. That's very good.

     Beat.

MAX   Wow. So do we play Name That Tune next? Scattergories? A little
     Pictionary? *(beat)* Seriously, I'm very busy, so…

SYLVIA   I need you to find someone for me, Max.

MAX   Try under the sofa. That's where I normally find things.

SYLVIA   It's not that simple.

MAX   Yah, it never is. Is this about the Chinese thing?

SYLVIA   That's a little vague.

---

2   "A Dialogue of Self and Soul," W.B. Yeats.

MAX   *I'm* being vague? That's like a—what is that?—black thing… calling the other black thing… black.

SYLVIA His name is Tommy Jade.

MAX   Never heard of him.

SYLVIA Well that's going to have to change.

MAX   How am I supposed to find a guy I never heard of?

SYLVIA I'll tell you where to look, Max. This isn't going to be difficult. Unless you make it difficult.

MAX   The fuck does that mean?

SYLVIA You start in Chinatown, Max. You go to Chinatown, and you find Tommy Jade.

> *She walks out the door. Beat. MAX grabs his heart and screams. He passes out again.*

Three: Tommy vs. The Dominion of Canada

> *1923. TOMMY Jade is talking to Mr. COOGAN, an immigration official. They meet in secret. Shadows play on their faces and their whispers are just barely audible. TOMMY has a paper bag clutched in his hand.*

COOGAN Tommy Jade.

TOMMY   That what they calling me.

COOGAN *Call* you—that's what— *(chuckling)* Jesus.

TOMMY   *(correcting him)* Tommy.

COOGAN I know.

> *TOMMY thrusts the bag at COOGAN.*

No! Don't—

He pushes it back.

—okay—no bag now.

TOMMY   Bag now?

He thrusts it again. Again, it is pushed back.

COOGAN   Whoa, easy there, friend. I know… I know you're excited to see your wifey again, but this is a big risk I'm taking for you.

COOGAN looks carefully around.

Okay, gimme the bag.

TOMMY is cautious now.

TOMMY   Bag?

COOGAN   Yah, gimme the—

TOMMY   Bag now?

COOGAN   Yes, Tommy, bag now.

TOMMY slowly moves the bag towards COOGAN. COOGAN takes it and rifles through the contents.

Six hundred?

TOMMY nods

Good man. Attaboy. Okay, so you understand, Tommy, this is five hundred for the tax, and one hundred for insurance. You understand insurance?

TOMMY   No.

COOGAN   I get her through immigration. Make sure. For this. Special favour. My friend.

TOMMY   Friend.

COOGAN   Yes, my friend, Tommy Jade.

TOMMY   Jesus.

COOGAN   Sure. This is good. Good work, my friend.

TOMMY   I tell Chor-swan to come?

COOGAN   No no no. Not yet. Um... how do I say this? We will find *(gesticulating largely) find*, we *find* her. In China. See, your wifey's appli— *(more gesticulating) application*... it was *rejected. (makes sad face)* So now *we*... go *different* way... to *bring* her to *Ca-na-da*. Yah? *(TOMMY looks confused.) Money* pay *tax*... *insurance* pay *intercontinental relocation fee. (Beat. COOGAN has confused himself.)* I don't... I don't have a gesture... for that. Do you understand?

    Beat.

TOMMY   I tell Chor-swan to come?

COOGAN   Jesus.

TOMMY   Tommy.

COOGAN   *(at a loss)* Six months. Okay? I need six months. Then we'll get your wifey here. One way or another.

    TOMMY thinks.

TOMMY   Six month. Okay.

COOGAN   Attaboy. August 1923. I promise.

TOMMY   Okay. *(Beat. He bows his head to COOGAN, a humble servant.)* Thank you.

COOGAN   Sure. Sure, Tommy. Now, just remember, okay? Government, *bad*. Coogan, *good*. Coogan, *friend*. But Coogan get in lots of trouble if anyone find out about this. Okay? So, don't tell—no tell, okay?

> *TOMMY presses his lips shut and smiles.*

Attaboy.

> *He gives TOMMY the thumbs up and walks out. TOMMY looks after him, then leaves in the opposite direction*

Four: Max vs. His Heart

> *MAX is in a hospital. A white DOCTOR is shining a light into his eyes.*

DOCTOR   Can you tell me your name?

MAX   Where am I? Where was I, just now?

DOCTOR   Your name.

MAX   Max Lochran.

DOCTOR   What do you do, Mr. Lochran?

MAX   I'm a—what is that—an attorney.

DOCTOR   Like Eric Peterson on *Street Legal*?

MAX   No, he was a—what a terrible—I'm the chief liaison with the Department of Justice. I handle settlements and—where am I?

DOCTOR   You're at Toronto General. You went into cardiac arrest, do you remember that?

MAX   At my office?

DOCTOR   At a strip club.

MAX   But I wasn't at a strip club today.

DOCTOR *(laughs)* You don't have to lie to me, Mr. Lochran, I'm not your wife.

MAX My wife is dead.

Beat.

DOCTOR Sorry. The ring…

MAX Yah. *(beat)* Look, I don't remember—

DOCTOR We often forget several moments, sometimes days, preceding an attack like yours. Sometimes people go into comas, Mr. Lochran, you should consider yourself lucky.

MAX What day is it?

DOCTOR Monday, the twenty-eighth.

MAX Today—it's still—that's today. I was in my office…

DOCTOR Mr. Lochran, it's okay. We all like strippers here. I was at the Brass Rail just this morning for the brunch buffet. I still need to ask you a few more questions to make sure you're not scrambled eggs up there and then you can go. Now: can you tell me how many fingers I'm holding up?

He gives MAX the finger.

MAX One.

DOCTOR Excellent. Now if *(He switches to Cantonese.)* Yue goh yow leung gah foah cheh, joy tung yut see ghan, yow but tung goh foah cheh jam hoi cheut, keu— *[Two trains leave from opposite stations, moving at equal speed—]*

MAX What? What did you say?

DOCTOR *(sighs)* Yue goh yow leung gah foah cheh, joy tung yut see ghan— *[Two trains leave from opposite stations—]*

MAX   English, can you say it in English?

DOCTOR   *(in English)* Mr. Lochran, I *am* speaking English. What are you hearing?

MAX   I don't know. It sounded... I don't know.

DOCTOR   I think we should probably keep you here for observation a little longer.

MAX   No, that's not possible. I have meetings, I—my son, I should get back to my—he's home alone. *(He starts pulling tubes out and disconnecting wires from his body.)* I need to go now—

DOCTOR   Mr. Lochran—

MAX   Where did they find me? A strip club, you said—but where?

    Beat.

DOCTOR   Chinatown, Max. They found you in Chinatown.

    MAX runs out of the hospital.

Five: Max vs. Danny

    MAX's home. DANNY is on the floor, a map spread out in front of him, markers in organized stacks. He is calculating MAX's route home. MAX walks in the door, on the phone mid-call.

MAX   This goddamn Chinese thing—we have to take a hard line, Bob, a hard line, or this country is going to the—what do you call those—the fucking barking things—the *dogs*, Bob.

    DANNY runs to MAX, map in hand.

Hold on a sec.

    He covers the mouthpiece of the phone and addresses DANNY quickly.

What is it, Danny?

DANNY   You took the wrong way home, Max. The wrong way. You didn't stay on the yellow line, you should have stayed on the yellow line.

MAX   Okay, Danny, just... I'm on the phone, so just... *(back to the phone)* Sorry, Bob. My kid is... I think I need to get a new nurse. Full-time, maybe. He's getting... I keep hoping he'll grow out of it. Just a—what is that—a phase, or something. But I don't think—

DANNY starts moaning. MAX is growing impatient.

I gotta go, Bob.

He hangs up the phone and addresses DANNY.

You happy now, Danny? I was on the phone and—what? What is it?

DANNY   You took the Don Valley Parkway, but you should take Yonge Street, always take Yonge Street, it's on the yellow line.

MAX   I like the DVP. There's something relaxing about moving that slowly. It's zen. Like a rock garden.

DANNY   It's on the red line, Max! The red line, you have to stay off the red line... *(He trails off, muttering and getting worked up.)*

MAX   Danny... *(no response)* Danny, look at me. *(no response)* Look at me, Danny, please. *(DANNY levels his eyes to MAX.)* What is this about? Is this about me coming home on time? Or... Danny?

DANNY   She was on the red line.

MAX   Who was?

DANNY   She went out on the red line and she never came back. She drove on the red line and it got crossed with another car's red line. And she never came back.

Beat. MAX is uncomfortable.

Promise to stay off the red line, Max. *(He shows MAX the map, a fractal diagram of yellow and red lines.)* Follow the yellow line. Promise.

MAX   We're not talking about this.

DANNY   Max...

MAX   You see Dr. Chao on Friday, okay? Talk to him about it. He can... he's more—what is that—equipped... for this. Okay? Just... show him the map. Let him deal with... *(beat)* What do you want for dinner? You want pizza? *(beat)* No. Of course you don't want—pizza is round, and you only eat square— *(Beat. MAX's frustration is getting the best of him.)* I mean, you can draw a fucking map of Toronto from *memory*, that's normal... but eating *round food*—that's a-a-a fucking... atrocity...

DANNY   Promise, Max.

MAX   *(exploding)* I don't want to talk about it!

Beat. DANNY sulks. MAX stares.

Why now? Why is this... today, why now?

Beat. DANNY looks at the floor. MAX suddenly remembers.

Jesus. Next week... five years. That's it, isn't it?

DANNY   Five is a prime number.

MAX   *(quietly)* I knew that. I knew that. I didn't...

Beat.

I'm sorry, Danny. I didn't mean to yell. You're okay... you're okay—we're okay.

DANNY   Okay.

MAX   I… you're a good boy, Danny.

DANNY   Okay.

> DANNY *gets under the table and picks up a Rubik's Cube.* MAX's *phone rings. He answers.*

MAX   Max Lochran. *(beat)* Right now? It's been a long day, I just—yah. Okay. Be there soon.

> *He hangs up, sighs, looks at* DANNY.

I… uh, forgot a book. At my office. I have to—

DANNY   Max—

MAX   I won't be long. Just… be good. It's seven o'clock, it's time for *Price is Right.* Watch your show and I'll—

DANNY   No, Max!

> DANNY *takes the Rubik's Cube and starts slamming it against the floor.*

MAX   Okay… okay… *okay!*

> DANNY *stops hitting the cube on the floor.*

Get your coat.

> *Without a word,* DANNY *grabs his coat, almost five sizes too large for him, and a big winter hat. He and* MAX *silently walk out the door.*

Six: Max vs. The Symbolic Agreement

> MAX *and* HATCH *are at a lawyer bar on Bay Street.* DANNY *sits between them, his hat still on, ignoring the two men, solving the Rubik's Cube.*

HATCH   A heart attack? Jesus, Max.

MAX   I'm fine. A little—but okay.

HATCH   My dad, he was a heart attack. Granddaddy, too. You gotta be careful, Max, these things are, like, programmed for us. We got no control, just… programmed. We all got an expiry date, Max, stamped on our insides. You gotta be careful. Keep the stress down, Max, no sudden jolts or— *(He jumps up and points behind MAX.)* WHAT THE FUCK IS THAT! *(MAX jumps up out of his chair with a yell, looks behind him. There's nothing there. HATCH laughs up a storm.)* I'm just fucking with you. You okay? Still tickin'? Yah, you'll be fine.

MAX   Fuck you, Hatch.

HATCH   Aw, don't be sore, Huck!

MAX   You drag me out tonight just for that?

HATCH   What? No. No, sugar plum. I "dragged you out" because I got a call on my *home line* from the representative for the Chinese Canadian National Council.

MAX   *(sighs)* She called you. She shouldn't have—what a bitch.

HATCH   They want more. A "symbolic" twenty-three million, or "recognition" for the descendants. They're accusing us—and I'm paraphrasing here—accusing us of waiting for most of them to die off before making reparations.

MAX   That's fucking ridiculous. Symbolic, a "symbolic"—what is that?

HATCH   It's a symbol, Max.

MAX   I'll give 'em a "symbolic"… I was at Dundas and Spadina last week, in Chinatown, right? Looking for a bank machine. Danny—

DANNY   Hi, Max.

MAX   Hi. *(continuing)* —wants some DVD or something—a hat maybe—it's not important. I need a bank machine. So I walk up to that RBC, you know that one on the corner there? I walk up and the screen, all the instructions, right... they're in Chinese. They're in fucking *Chinese*. At the Royal Bank of *Canada*, Hatch. Of *Canada*, and it's in—I mean *that's* a symbol, it's a sign of—what is that—the times, or something.

HATCH   Couldn't you just switch it to English? There's a button for English.

MAX   It's the *principle* of it. It's that we're in Canada; Chinese isn't the official language of Canada, English is. And French, I guess, but who even speaks that anymore? Even so, even so, if it was French on the screen, I could handle that. I just *choisir anglais* or whatever, how am I supposed to know what to do with a bunch of pictographs?

HATCH   I'm pretty sure there's a button for English. It says "English."

MAX   They're taking over. They study harder in school, they work harder, and then they bring each other up the ladder because who knows, right? My wife's brother! Perfect example: working the rice paddies in China one minute, not a word of English, a quick boat ride later he's CFO of Merrill-fucking-Lynch. The fuck is that? And I'm not being racist, here, I love Oriental girls! I married one, they're fucking sexy as hell... nothing wrong with that. But they take over and you don't even notice. And now they want—what?—twenty-three mil for something they never even had to go through? It's not like they suffered for it. Christ...

HATCH   Watch your blood pressure, Max.

MAX   It pisses me off...

HATCH   I know. Look, these CCNC people... they're annoying. They're worse than poor people. Honestly. Begging for table scraps, pulling at our sleeves and then... *blaming* us for—y'know? They don't get it—we are trying to help! *We're* the good guys here! But these things take time. There's due process to be—well *you* understand... they want an answer today and I can't give them one. We keep bringing things to the table, and they keep screaming "not good enough."

MAX   An open negotiation is—

HATCH   I'm not finished. The problem, Max, is the longer and louder
        they scream… the more likely that people are going to listen.
        And we can't have that. We've done informal surveys, only 23%
        of Canadians even know what this redress business is *about*. That's
        77% of the general public—real Canadians—who don't even
        know what the fucking Head Tax *was*! But the longer these peo-
        ple scream "not good enough"… the greater chance somebody
        is gonna stop and ask "not good enough for what?" And that's the
        beginning of the end, Max. This is our chance to acknowledge
        and commemorate a tragic part of our nation's history, but more
        importantly it's our last chance to do it on *our* terms. They want
        us to "apologize," to claim "liability." How will that look, Max?
        You tell me how that will look.

MAX   I guess it would—

HATCH   Like a dirty sanchez. A dirty sanchez on the face of Canada, Max.
        How fucking grotesque is that?

MAX   Pretty… grotesque.

HATCH   Keep her quiet. Just a little while longer, just until we've run
        some numbers and can find a *fair* and *equitable* agreement. *(beat)*
        Or a loophole. Whichever comes first. Tell her anything you have
        to. Tell her we'll consider the twenty-three mil if you have to, just
        get the town crier down from the hill. You feel me?

MAX   I… um… I feel you.

HATCH   Could you remind her of something as well, gumdrop?

MAX   Sure.

HATCH   Remind her that if she ever calls me at home again, I will cut off
        your dick and shove it down her throat.

        Threatening beat.

Clear?

MAX nods. HATCH smiles.

We met on the level.

MAX   And we depart on the square.

HATCH   Good meeting.

HATCH prepares to leave.

MAX   Hey, d'you shake that thing?

HATCH   What thing?

MAX   The one a few weeks back, cops caught you with a… y'know, a—what is that—the money and the sex?

HATCH   Oh, the hooker. Yah, that was almost a thing.

MAX   What'd you do?

HATCH   I said, "Officer, you've got it all wrong. I haven't given this woman any money for sex." Cop looks at the table, asks me: "Yah, what's the three hundred bucks for?" I look him dead in the eye and tell him: "The condom."

They laugh.

I gave him a pass on this racial profiling thing he was up against, so we're cool now. We're gonna hit up Brass Rail tomorrow night, you want in?

MAX   I don't know.

HATCH   Oh, don't worry about him, he looks the other way. Besides, mileage at the Rail is pretty low. You wanna decent hand job you gotta go up by the airport.

MAX   I told... uh, Danny—

> *Cued by his name being spoken,* DANNY *speaks but doesn't look up and continues solving the cube.*

DANNY   Hi, Max.

MAX   Uh... hi—I told Danny—

DANNY   Hi, Max.

MAX   Hi. Well, I told him I would be home for dinner tomorrow.

DANNY   We're having lasagna.

MAX   We... yes, because... it's square. He likes square food.

HATCH   *(without even the sensitivity for an aside to* MAX*)* Hey, is he still retarded or did he grow out of that?

MAX   He's, well he's not... not actually *retarded*.

HATCH   He's got autism, doesn't he? *(*MAX *nods.)* My uncle had autism. He was retarded. *(He pats* DANNY *on his head.)* Anyway, get a sitter or— better yet—put on *Rain Man* for him or something. Sneak out. Use the sitter money for lap dances. Hehe... "sitter money"... lap dances... that shit's funny. Be there at nine.

> *He tosses that last line over his shoulder as he strides through the door and is gone.* MAX *tries to argue, but he's already out and in his car.* MAX *sighs, puts on his coat and takes* DANNY's *arm.*

MAX   C'mon, Danny.

> DANNY *isn't finished the cube yet. He wrenches his arm free from* MAX *with a loud moan. He continues solving the cube.* MAX *sits down. He hails a waitress.*

Another bourbon. *(beat)* Bring the bottle.

MAX hangs his head over the table. He does not hear DANNY when he speaks.

DANNY   "He with body waged a fight,
But body won; it walks upright.
Then he struggled with the heart;
Innocence and peace depart.
Then he struggled with the mind;
His proud heart he left behind.
Now his wars on God begin;
At stroke of midnight God shall win."[3]

> *DANNY solves the cube. He smiles, then slams it down on the floor. Coloured cubes scatter everywhere.*

Seven: Sylvia vs. Max's Nerves

MAX's office. He is on the phone with the CCNC.

MAX   Yah, Linda; my dick, your throat—that's what he said. Now, unless amputative fellatio really does it for you, you will delete that goddamn number from your goddamn speed-dial. *(beat)* Goddammit. I'll say it again: the feds are *considering* meeting your request for a symbolic twenty-three million. It's not on the table. It's not anywhere near the table. *(beat)* I don't know, it's on a shelf across the room from the table, at the risk of pushing this metaphor too far. But if I find out you went over my head again, you're going to end up with twenty bucks and another Canadian Heritage commercial, you feel me? *(puffing up his chest for the phone's benefit)* I'm Max Lochran. I play golf with the Attorney General. Max Lochran does that. I don't even know your last name.

> *He hangs up. He kicks his feet up and cracks open another bottle of bourbon.*

I don't want to see anything Chinese for at least a week.

> *Beat. SYLVIA enters silently. She clears her throat and MAX starts.*

3   "Four Stages of Man," W.B. Yeats.

You.

SYLVIA   Surprised to see me?

MAX   No, I just... I thought I locked the door.

SYLVIA   You did.

      Beat.

MAX   Okay.

SYLVIA   You look tired. Rough night?

MAX   What are you doing here? What do you want?

SYLVIA   I'm the same as anyone, Mr. Lochran. I want justice.

MAX   Well, you're in the right department.

SYLVIA   I thought I might be. *(She licks her lips.)* How is your search coming?

MAX   My...? Oh, your—the "Tommy Jade" thing. *(beat)* I got nothing.

SYLVIA   That's not very encouraging.

MAX   I'm very busy.

SYLVIA   Aren't you curious?

MAX   I *was* curious. Thought there might be something to you. Something more than just long legs and dead Irish poets. So I got Some Intern to do a bit of research. She found... *(He pulls out a sheet of velum with Chinese characters on it.)* this. A letter or something. This was buried in discovery from the 2002 class-action suit. It is dated 1923 and it is signed—I'm told—"Tommy Jade." *(Beat. He slaps the paper on the table.)* He's dead. And I'm not curious anymore.

SYLVIA   May I?

MAX nods and she takes the letter carefully in hand.

Did you read it?

MAX   It's in Chinese.

SYLVIA You didn't even try?

MAX   Look, you wanna talk about the redress, fine. You wanna buy me
        a drink, even better. But I pretty much draw the line at shooting
        the breeze over a dead man's diary entry.

SYLVIA Everything is connected.

MAX   Sure.

        Beat.

SYLVIA Where did you find it?

MAX   Discovery.

        SYLVIA stares at him blankly. MAX sighs, he explains it for her.

        It was documentation we obtained from the CCNC for the class
        action they brought against the federal government. They were
        requesting reparations for the Head Tax and Exclusion Act, and
        that would have been supporting—what is that—evidence, or
        something.

SYLVIA Who won the suit?

MAX   No one *won*, that's not how it works…

SYLVIA So tell me how it works.

MAX   The case never made it to trial. Your people couldn't prove that
        what the government did was unjust.

SYLVIA My people?

MAX   You know what I mean. Unfair, yes. Regrettable, sure. But not unjust. The federal government didn't—technically—didn't break any laws.

SYLVIA   So you regard it as *just*. As an act of justice.

MAX   Not "of," "*with*," we acted *with*... justice.

SYLVIA   And now...

MAX   Now, we admit that it was a—what is that—a terrible thing. And we make amends. We give you a... like, a *thing*... a monetary *thing*—an *amount*. We give you that. Tax free, mind you. Which is... ironic, I understand... but—well, it's *fair*. We're even now.

SYLVIA   Even?

MAX   Okay, not *even*, but—

SYLVIA   Is that what your apology says?

MAX   No! *(beat)* Kind of. *(beat)* We are righting a historical wrong.

SYLVIA   You're making it right?

MAX   We are.

SYLVIA   How?

MAX   By acknowledging—

SYLVIA   Acknowledging?

MAX   Well, *recognizing*—

SYLVIA   Recognizing.

MAX   Stop repeating what I say in a contemptuous tone—

SYLVIA   Do you accept responsibility for it?

MAX   Me personally?

SYLVIA   This country.

MAX   It's not about liability.

SYLVIA   Yes. It is.

Beat.

MAX   *(quietly)* We do not accept liability.

Beat.

SYLVIA   Do you believe it was just?

MAX   The Head Tax? The...? It's a moot point, that decision's been—

SYLVIA   Do you believe... it was just?

MAX   I believe in the law.

SYLVIA   *(hands the letter back to MAX)* Tommy wrote this letter to his wife in China. It never made it out of the country. *(She hands it back to him.)* Read.

MAX   I don't read Chinese.

SYLVIA   Do your best.

MAX   *(at a loss, he stares at the page)* I don't know... um... *(He switches to Cantonese.)* Chor San. *(English)* Heh. That's weird, I can...

(He continues in Cantonese.) Chor San... Yee gah hai bwoon yeah sam deem jung. Yut chay doo ting dunne sai. Gnoah hai lee goah yun ghan teen tong—seah seun bey lay. Dan hai dong gnoah heung cheeen mong... jing hai fat yeen... hung heu... tung my jick mok. *[Dear Love. It's three in the morning and life has stopped. I write to you, from the end of the world, from the edge of the horizon... only to tell you there is nothing beyond. Only emptiness.]*

From behind him, TOMMY Jade appears and begins translating in English. His voice soon takes over.

TOMMY   And behind me, a sea of broken promises. Today is a special day here. July first, Dominion Day. Humiliation Day. The Dominion of Canada passed a new law this morning. An exclusion law. We are no longer welcome on these shores.

The man who told me said it was for the good of Canada. Too many Chinese means that white people will have too few jobs. I think we have outlived our usefulness.

I will not see you this fall. Or the fall after that. You will never see these barracks from which I write to you. You will never see the pen I have used every night. Or the hand that holds it. I'll continue to send you my wages, everything I can spare. But I fear this is my last letter to you.

Last night I dreamt I was the ocean. Infinite and ever-reaching, I could be on these shores and on yours at once. This morning I awoke to find—I am no such thing.

TOMMY fades out. MAX switches back to English.

MAX   I remain, your orphan love,

Tommy Jade.

He puts down the letter. He stares, dumbfounded, at SYLVIA.

SYLVIA   Does that sound "just" to you?

MAX   How did I do that?

SYLVIA   We're capable of all sorts of things, Mr. Lochran.

MAX sits, his head spinning like a top. He automatically takes a bottle of bourbon from his drawer and pours himself a double. He downs it. He pours another.

(A realization. A confirmation.) He loved her.

MAX   What?

SYLVIA Tommy. He loved his wife. More than anything. *(She looks at him.)*
You stole that from him.

MAX   *I* didn't do anything to him.

SYLVIA You need to find him.

MAX   He's *dead*, lady. I can't find him if he's *dead*.

> Beat. SYLVIA *takes a letter opener off* MAX's *desk. She fingers the blade
> reminiscently, dangerously.*

SYLVIA "Still razor-keen, still like a looking glass
Unspotted by the centuries."[4]

> *She spins the letter opener around and drives it through* MAX's *hand,
> pinning him to the desk. He screams.*

MAX   Oh *come on*——

SYLVIA Are you listening now, Max?

MAX   My fucking hand...

> *She twists the opener, corkscrewing his hand. He screams again.*

SYLVIA I find men respond best to pain... to think I used to ply them
with sex...

MAX   *(wryly)* Ah, the good old days.

SYLVIA This world is full of things people don't understand. I don't understand how you can sleep at night given what you do in the
safety of the day, and you don't understand how you can find a
man who's been dead for eighty years. But I know you sleep at

---

4   "A Dialogue of Self and Soul," W.B. Yeats.

night, so you're just going to have to believe this is actually happening to you. Are we clear?

> *MAX nods. SYLVIA pulls the letter opener out, MAX winces and pulls his tie off to wrap around his hand.*

MAX You got anger issues, sister.

SYLVIA Sylvia.

MAX Huh?

SYLVIA My name is Sylvia. Not "sister." I'm not... not your sister.

MAX Sylvia what?

> *She glares at him.*

Okay, just "Sylvia" then. Like Madonna. Or Satan.

SYLVIA You want to know who I am?

MAX It's crossed my mind.

SYLVIA The place they found you, before you got to the hospital...

MAX The strip club?

SYLVIA You need to go back, see what's there.

MAX Strippers, I imagine.

SYLVIA It's called the Golden Pearl. Go back. See for yourself. And then you find Tommy.

> *She walks out the door. MAX calls after her.*

Hey, I want my letter opener back!

She throws it behind her back, it sinks deep into MAX's thigh. He cries out and falls to the ground clutching it. He yells after her.

Oh, that's cute! Real mature!

He removes it and tosses it to the ground.

These are three hundred dollar pants...

Eight: Max vs. The Peep Show

The Golden Pearl, a strip club in Chinatown. Women dance on poles and shooter girls hover over tables with long legs and short skirts. The girls, not the tables. MAX drinks a double of bourbon from a dirty glass, alone. His hand and thigh are both tied and bloody, he limps when he walks. The owner, WILLY Chan, approaches from behind.

WILLY   Mr. Lochran?

MAX   Mr....?

WILLY   Chan. I am the owner of the Golden Pearl.

MAX   Right. Chan. Like "Smith" or something over there, isn't it?

WILLY   Smith is like Smith. Chan is like Chan.

MAX   Common, I mean.

WILLY   I know what you mean. But, Mr. Lochran, I'm sure you will agree that nothing here is... common.

MAX   Yah, whatever, pal. Look. Have you seen me before?

WILLY   Before today, you mean?

MAX   Before right now. Like, Monday, did you see me here Monday?

WILLY   You look like you need a drink, Mr. Lochran. And perhaps an ambulance.

MAX   I have a drink. I'll get to the ambulance.

WILLY   A real drink, then? Our bourbon is watered down at best, but I can offer you a fine vodka tonic. Or a girl, maybe, for our VIP room? If your tastes are a bit more... exotic, I can offer you some lovely illicit narcotics. Meth? Opium? Bombay Black? Though I can't recommend the latter, it was never to my liking.

MAX   Just answers, Chan. I had a heart attack earlier this week and the doc says I was found here. But I don't remember being here before today. Can you explain that?

WILLY   Sounds like you've had a rough week.

MAX   I expect it to get worse. So give it up, Chan. You seen me here before, or do I need to get a coupl'a RCMP types down here?

DANNY walks in the door and approaches MAX.

Danny...

DANNY   Hi, Max. I'm thirsty.

MAX   Chan, this is my son Danny.

DANNY   Wei, deem ah? *[How's it going?]*

WILLY   Eh. Gum seung ha la. *[Eh, you know. Same old.]* You bring your child into a place like this?

MAX   What? No! What kinda father d'you think I am? *(beat)* I left him in the car. *(beat)* Was that Chinese?

DANNY   I'm thirsty, Max.

WILLY   *(to the bartender, off)* Wei, Julio, fai dee heu loah booie lie-cha bey goh lang jai laaa! *[Julio, bring the boy a milk tea!]*

DANNY   M'goi sai, Julio. *[Thank you, Julio.]*

WILLY   We will take care of the boy.

MAX   Where did he learn—

WILLY   You were here. You wanted to see the peep show. But you couldn't get in.

MAX   Why couldn't I get in?

WILLY   You didn't know the password.

MAX   What's the password?

WILLY   If I told you that, it wouldn't be a password.

MAX   Can I see the peep show now?

WILLY   Do you know the password?

> *Beat.* MAX *is about to give up when* DANNY *answers for him.*

DANNY   Sylvia.

WILLY   Mr. Lochran. Welcome to the peep show.

MAX   How did—

> WILLY *ushers* MAX *past a curtain into another room. It's a standard peep show. A curtain covers a glass booth. A chair is in front of it, with a jar next to it.* MAX *sits in the chair.*

Okay... let's do this. Where do I put the money?

WILLY   Mr. Lochran, this is not an ordinary peep show. You are seeking answers, are you not?

MAX   You could say that.

WILLY   The show will reveal those answers to you. But payment is... well, some find the price too steep.

MAX   I can cover it.

WILLY   So you're saying you will pay the price...

MAX   Yah. Sure, whatever.

WILLY   Very well. We are now in a contract. I am the agent of collection and you are the debtor. Do you understand?

MAX   Just tell me where I put the quarter and get this thing started, would'ya, Chan?

WILLY   Very well. But we don't use quarters here. We deal in truth. Truth and justice. The word of truth comes from the mouth of justice, Mr. Lochran, isn't that so?

MAX   You get that from a fortune cookie?

WILLY   You are the mouthpiece of justice, Mr. Lochran. And you owe me the truth. As an agent of collection, it is my job to obtain it. Please understand, it's nothing personal.

He takes vice grips from an unseen pocket and is swiftly upon MAX. He puts up a fight, but is no match for the old man. The vice grips go into MAX's mouth, and with a scream, a tooth is extracted. WILLY drops it into the jar.

MAX   Jesus Christ! The fuck are you—

Payment received, the curtain lifts to reveal a home in 1943. MAX watches, as if through a window.

Nine: Sylvia vs. The Policeman

1943. SYLVIA is in the home of STRYKER, a lieutenant with the RCMP. He is drunk. She is wearing a vintage red dress, seductive and terrifying, she stalks him with a slow dance.

STRYKER   Dance. Dance like you dance in the emperor's chambers. Dance like China dances. For me.

SYLVIA   Yes, master.

STRYKER "Master." I like that. You Oriental girls really know your place.
Don't you?

SYLVIA   Yes, master.

STRYKER Not like your men. Your men... who *infect* pure Canadian wom-
en. You understand "pure"? Pedigrew.

SYLVIA   Pedig*ree*.

STRYKER That's what I said. Last year, in '42, there were ten cases of white
women found drugged on opium. This year? Twenty-five. *Twenty-
five!* Something needed to change, you hear? And I was the one
who changed it. You know what I did? As a lieutenant of the honourable RCMP, I took away their walls. I can go—without *warrant*,
little miss—I can go into any chink's home, their laundry shops,
their restaurants, and I can find their opium and the trinkets they
use to lure white women into their back parlours, where chinks
drug and rape them. I rescued my people from a terrible fate.
A world full'a... mongrels. Half-breeds. Mutts. Nothing worse
than a mutt.

SYLVIA   *(biting her tongue)* You are so... heroic.

STRYKER I don't wanna brag or nothing. But, yes, I am like a god. Like an
angel. An angel of vengeance, and I will *strike down* the yellow
peril. To protect. To save. To... that's what God wants me to do.
That's my utility.

SYLVIA   Utility. I like that word.

STRYKER I bet you do.

         She runs her finger down his chest.

SYLVIA   Very important man. Picture in the paper man. Protector man.

         She drops a strap from her shoulder and coquettishly curls her leg.

Maybe... I can help you relax.

She lifts her dress up to her thigh. Unseen, she palms a letter opener in her hand.

STRYKER   Mmm...

She begins to undo his shirt. She slips his handcuffs off his belt and dangles them in front of him.

SYLVIA   Now... what's my purpose?

STRYKER   You're my little chinky whore.

SYLVIA   Oh yes. And who owns me?

STRYKER   I own you...

SYLVIA   Yes.

STRYKER   C'mere!

He grabs her face and pulls it close to kiss her, but stops. He presses open her eyes and pushes her away in disgust.

Christ Almighty. You're one'a them! A mongrel! Get out!!

He tries to jump up but realizes he has been handcuffed to the chair.

Hey...

SYLVIA slides the police baton from his belt and wields it expertly. She spins it easily, rolls it over her hand, descending upon him like a cat about to bat around a mouse.

SYLVIA   Call me a mongrel again.

STRYKER   You filthy mutt, I'll—

She cracks the baton across his face. He spits a mouthful of blood at her.

Half-breed—

She rams the baton into his stomach. More blood.

Useless. Mistake. You'll never be one of us!

She smiles and breaks his kneecap with the baton.

SYLVIA   I don't want to be one of you.

STRYKER   Yah… but you'll never be one of them, either.

> *Beat. This hurts SYLVIA as much as any words could. She drops the baton on the floor and fingers the letter opener.*

SYLVIA   "Mere anarchy is loosed upon the world,
           The blood-dimmed tide is loosed, and everywhere
           The ceremony of innocence is drowned."[5]

STRYKER   The hell is that?

> *Beat.*

SYLVIA   My utility.

> *She wields the letter opener, and with one swift motion, slits the policeman's throat.*

Ten: Max vs. The Night

2006. MAX wakes up in the middle of the night, screaming. He looks around. He is alone. He rubs his eyes. He coughs. Something in his throat. He coughs again and spits out a tooth. Blood starts running from his mouth.

MAX   Jesus.

---

5   "The Second Coming," W.B. Yeats.

He goes to wash out his mouth. DANNY *comes into his room. He sits on the bed.* MAX *comes back in, a Kleenex shoved in his mouth, he sees* DANNY *and cries out.*

Fuck! Sorry, Danny—Danny? You scared—what are you—did I wake you?

DANNY   What's wrong?

MAX   Nothing, just—a bad dream, it was—a bad dream.

> MAX *crawls back into bed,* DANNY *next to him.*

DANNY   "The darkness drops again; but now I know
that twenty centuries of stony sleep
Were vexed to nightmare by a rocking cradle."[6]

> *Pause.*

MAX   Where did you learn that?

> DANNY *points to the door.*

DANNY   She told me.

MAX looks up to see SYLVIA *in a red dress standing in the doorway. She is wielding the blood-stained letter opener.*

2006. MAX *wakes up in the middle of the night, screaming. He looks around.* DANNY *and* SYLVIA *are gone. He spits the blood-soaked Kleenex out.*

Eleven: Max vs. The DJ

MAX is in Chinatown. Fruit stands and trash bags litter the streets. Hustle and bustle. Cantonese shoots like dice down the sidewalk and MAX is lost. He approaches vendors, shopkeepers and pedestrians.

---

6   "The Second Coming," W.B. Yeats.

MAX   Excuse me—um—hi there, excuse me… Have you seen a—
I'm looking for a man named Tommy Jade. Do you know a man
named Tommy Jade? I'm looking for Tommy Jade. Hello? Are
you—do you—have you—can you—hello? Can I ask you a—I
need to find—hey are those nectarines? I'll take one. Thanks.
Have you seen—hey, where are you—

*MAX sighs, his shoulders slump. He bites into the nectarine. Finally
he hears a voice speaking English, he turns towards it.*

HAPPY   …so we're gonna kick off the drive at five with a little Faye Wong.
Faye's gonna see you home safe with her version of "Dreams" by
the Cranberries.

*MAX turns a corner to see where the voice is coming from. It is HAPPY
Chan, an Asian guy between sixteen and thirty-five wearing a toque
and scrubs. He has a Discman in his hand with a wire running from
it into his backpack. The backpack is bulky and has a very long radio
antenna protruding up to the sky. He has a microphone headset on
with large headphones, which run into the backpack as well. Also a
belt full of switches and flashing lights.*

Don't rage on the road, listeners. Listen to this shit, it's hype, I'll
be back with traffic in a sec.

*He flips a switch on his belt and pushes a button on the Discman.
He dances a little. He breaks out a copy of the novel* Banana Boys,
and begins reading. MAX approaches him.

MAX   Excuse me.

No response.

Pardon me…

No response. He reaches out and touches HAPPY's arm, startling him.

HAPPY   Yo, don't touch me, man, I don't know you!

MAX   Sorry… sorry—I'm sorry.

HAPPY   Scared the shit outta me. Thought you was the Man.

MAX   The—what man?

HAPPY   Bitch, you know. The Man. Thought you was him. You ain't him?

MAX   I honestly don't have a clue what you're—

HAPPY   Whatever, man, can't you see I'm reading?

MAX   Sorry, I'm—

HAPPY   I was gonna wait for the movie, but you know adaptations… usually turn out to be shit. Fuck it, what you want, man?

MAX   I'm looking for a man named Tommy Jade. *(He eyes HAPPY up and down.)* Who the hell are you supposed to be?

HAPPY   I'm Happy Chan, the one-man radio station. You heard of me, right? Right.

MAX   Chan. Good, you're Chinese—that's good.

HAPPY   Bitch, I'm 1/5 Chinese, 1/7 Japanese, 3/8 Korean, 1/10 Filipino, 2/5 Taiwanese, 1/9 Laotian, 5/16 Mongolian and 3/4 Vietnamese. Chinese… I'm the whole goddamn Pacific Rim. Hold on, I gotta do a break.

       He flips a switch on his belt and swings the microphone over his mouth.

That was Faye Wong, listeners. She got an all right voice, but mostly I just like watching her videos on mute, know what I mean? Whatever. Now the traffic report for all you commuters out there.

       He looks around at the busy street.

Traffic's fucked. Don't take Spadina, don't go west on Dundas neither. Um…

He covers the microphone and addresses MAX.

Hey, you been down Bathurst?

MAX   What? I—it's fine, I guess—

HAPPY   *(back on the mic)* The white guy in front of me says take Bathurst. But he white, so he probably lying. Bitch. Next traffic in ten minutes. You're listening to 108.3 HAPY FM, Radio Free Toronto, the one-man radio station. Next up... *(He loads a CD into his Discman.)* we got Jin Tha Emcee, AKA 100 Grand Jin, with the track "Kill Whitey" on HAPY Radio, 108.3.

> *He pushes a button on the Discman, flips a switch on his belt and swings the microphone away.*

Sorry. You wanna talk to Tommy Jade?

> MAX *comes back.*

MAX   You know him?

HAPPY   Tommy Jade's dead, my friend. Dead and buried, like the rest of 'em.

MAX   I know... look, I know how it sounds... But I was told—someone said I could find him here. In Chinatown.

HAPPY   Who told you that?

MAX   Sylvia.

> HAPPY's *eyes widen.*

Does that name—

HAPPY   Bitch, did you just say you was talking to Sylvia?

MAX   Yah, why, you know her?

HAPPY   Shit. Keep your voice down, man. We gotsta go somewhere private and talk.

> *He shuffles a few feet to the left.* MAX *looks at him.* HAPPY *signals* MAX *to come over.* MAX *shuffles over to meet him.*

A'ight, we safe here. Bitch, you got yourself trouble if the lady in the red dress is making house calls.

MAX   What kind of trouble? What is this? She said she would—

HAPPY   *(covers his ears to shut* MAX *out)* Yo! I don't know what you're rolled up in, and I don't wanna know. But I know Tommy Jade been looking for Sylvia.

MAX   He's dead! How can he look for—he's *dead.*

HAPPY   *(looks* MAX *up and down)* Yah, I think you best be talking to the man himself. Hold up.

> *He flips a switch.*

S'up listeners, time to take a commercial break. I gotta switch frequencies, so y'all switch stations and listen to some commercials. S'all they play, motherfucking capitalist bitches. Back in two minutes. Peace outside.

> *He flips a switch, then another, and turns some dials.*

Okay, crackerjack, you got one minute with the man and then I lose the frequency.

> *He hands* MAX *a sheet of paper.*

Sign this.

MAX   What is it?

HAPPY   S'a liability waiver. Says I'm not responsible for anything I may do while under the influence here.

MAX   Have you been drinking?

HAPPY   A little. But I ain't talking 'bout that kinda influence. Sign, bitch.

          MAX signs the paper and hands it back.

          Okay. You ready?

MAX   For what?

          HAPPY smiles and flips a switch on his belt. The rest of the world disappears. There is no sound but MAX's breathing. HAPPY becomes TOMMY Jade.

TOMMY   Hello?

MAX   Hi.

TOMMY   Who this? Coogan?

MAX   What? What is this, some kinda joke?

TOMMY   Who are you?

MAX   Who are *you*?

TOMMY   I am Tommy Jade.

MAX   Right. Look, I'm really not in the mood for—just stop with this.

TOMMY   You stop. What you want?

MAX   Jesus!

TOMMY   Tommy!

MAX   I don't know if Sylvia put you up to—

TOMMY   Sylvia? You—you know Sylvia? I looking for—

MAX She's going to—Sylvia is going to do—I don't know—something bad, unless I can find Tommy Jade. What does that mean, does that mean something?

TOMMY You must help.

MAX How? What can I do?

TOMMY She will stop at nothing. So you must also stop at nothing.

MAX For what—to do what?

TOMMY She is confused. What she seeks is not justice.

MAX She said that, she said she wanted that.

TOMMY Not justice. Not anymore. Now she has only one purpose. One fixation.

MAX What does she want?

Beat.

TOMMY Vengeance.

Beat.

MAX How do I stop her?

TOMMY Find…

Static. A streetcar bell. The world is coming back. TOMMY's lips move but no words come out.

MAX What? You're cutting out—what?

TOMMY Tell Sylvia—

A car horn. People chattering. A cellphone rings.

MAX   I can't—

TOMMY   You can—

> *Tires screech. A plane passes overhead.*

> *A moment of clarity.*

> Find the white snake.

> *The world returns.* HAPPY *is back.* MAX *is confused.*

MAX   The white snake?

HAPPY   You wanna request Whitesnake? Do I look like Q107, bitch?

MAX   What happened, what was that?

HAPPY   That was the power of radio, my friend. Radio Free Toronto, HAPY FM...

> *He flips a switch and grabs the microphone.*

...is *back* on the air, sorry for the wait, I got some white guy with me, and he's just *blown away* by his first transcendental radio experience with the one and only, the inimitable, Tommy-fucking-Jade! A few words, honky?

> *He shoves the microphone in* MAX's *face.*

MAX   Huh?

HAPPY   How's Tommy doing, does he have any tips on the afterlife? What to pack, do they got cable, shit like that?

MAX   Find the white snake. Does that mean something?

HAPPY   *(pause)* Nope. Sounds like some fortune-cookie bullshit. Sorry. I think I know a guy who can help, though. My brother. He runs the one-man TV station in old Chinatown. You should see him!

MAX   No, this is—I can't do this. I've played your little—no, I'm being set—no, I can't—I won't—

HAPPY   Bitch, finish a fuckin' sentence.

MAX   Fuck it. I'm through with this shit, I'm done.

He leaves. HAPPY calls after him.

HAPPY   Hey! Hold up!

MAX stops. HAPPY saunters over to him, looks over his shoulder and speaks to him confidentially.

Yo, you obviously ain't got much experience here so I'm gonna go off the record. I'm philharmonic like that.

MAX   Philanthropic.

HAPPY   Don't use your fancy white words on me. Now you might be all "Bitch, I'm done with Sylvia." But Sylvia, man… she ain't done wit' you. You gotsta do your homework. Find out what you dealin' with.

MAX   How?

HAPPY   What, you want all the answers? How 'bout I just tell you who really killed Biggie while I'm at it? *Homework*, motherfucker. Read a goddamn newspaper.

Beat.

Run along, Missum Daisy, you're fucking up my chi.

Beat. MAX runs off. HAPPY looks after him.

Bitch.

Twelve: Danny vs. The Abduction

MAX's house. MAX isn't at home. DANNY is watching television and ar-
ranging household items in order of shape, then colour, then height.
He is watching The Price is Right, *and getting all of the answers*
correct.

TV   So, Helen, for the round-trip vacation to Maui, the windsurf-
            ing lessons and the scuba gear... within a thousand dollars, how
            much do you think this all costs?

DANNY $5,893.

TV   Bob, I'm going to say $3,400...

DANNY   You lose.

TV   Actual retail price: $5,893... sorry, Helen.

DANNY   Sorry, Helen.

            SYLVIA enters silently. She stands behind DANNY for some time, watch-
            ing him. DANNY senses her.

Where's Nurse George?

            SYLVIA doesn't answer. DANNY turns around slowly. He takes her in.

You're like the story said.

            She cocks her head to one side, finding DANNY curious. She un-
            sheathes her knife from its hidden place and begins slowly advanc-
            ing upon him. DANNY sticks his ground and closes his eyes, reciting:

"In cloud-pale rags, or in lace,
The rage-driven, rage-tormented, and rage-hungry troop,
Trooper belabouring trooper, biting at arm or at face,
Plunges towards nothing, arms and fingers spreading wide
For the embrace of nothing; and I, my wits astray
Because of all that senseless tumult, all but cried."

She is almost upon him. He opens his eyes, terror fills them.

"For vengeance on the murderers of…"[7]

She's got him.

MAX!

Thirteen: Max vs. Hatch

The Brass Rail. 2006. MAX and HATCH are drinking. MAX winces as his bourbon washes over the exposed nerve where his tooth used to be. He is unravelling.

HATCH   So you had a bad dream.

MAX   It wasn't a dream, Hatch.

HATCH   You woke up in bed.

MAX   Missing a—what is that—the biting thing—a tooth, Hatch. My tooth was—

HATCH   You're getting old, Maxie. Body's falling apart. Better get used to it.

MAX   I got my fucking tooth ripped out!

HATCH   I'll give you the number for my dentist. She's lukewarm, but the dental hygienists, Max… Christ, they make me feel young again. They undo the top button from their smocks, y'know… to distract you while they work.

MAX   And this girl, Hatch… she killed him, right there in cold blood.

HATCH   *(bored and in disbelief)* In the peep show.

MAX   But it wasn't a peep show, it was a… I don't know what it was. But it happened. And then this radio kid… he said she'd stop at nothing—

---

7   "Meditations in Time of Civil War," W.B. Yeats.

HATCH   You said yourself you'd already killed half a bottle of bourbon—

MAX   It happened. *(He pulls out some newspaper printouts from his bag.)* Look. The *Toronto Star* has archives going back to 1894. The quality is… terrible, but you can see… *(He points to a picture.)* Robert Stryker, the guy looked just like this. "RCMP Lieutenant killed in his home." This is—I saw this.

HATCH   Max, that happened in 1943. You probably saw it on *Cold Case* or something. C'mon, let's get a lap dance. I'm buying.

MAX   There's more.

> *Reams of paper spill out over the floor. There are years and years worth of newspaper printouts.*

> *Stray pieces are sticking to MAX's bloody hands.*

HATCH   Christ, Max. Have you slept?

MAX   I slept on Sunday.

HATCH   It's *Wednesday*.

MAX   Just, *look*. These are violent crimes—homicides—for the last century. I cross-referenced… *(He shuffles papers around, getting paper cut after paper cut, the sheets are a bloody mess.)* look, I mean… people, killed in the same way, the same manner, all of them involved in some degree of anti-Chinese activity—spanning decades—*decades*, Hatch. Seventy years. How is that—I mean, what is this? Right? This girl… she couldn't 've been over twenty. I mean, Asians, right, it's hard to tell—but still…

> *HATCH has had enough. He puts on his lawyer face and stares MAX dead in the eye.*

HATCH   She was Chinese. This girl you saw?

MAX   *(correcting)* Biracial.

HATCH   *(recorrecting)* Chinese. Like your wife.

MAX   Hatch...

HATCH   You miss her, Max, that's normal. Especially now. Five years ago, wasn't it? Almost to the day? Anniversary grief. That's a biggie. And it's common, under these circumstances... you think you see them. Everywhere. Y'know? Just last week I saw this guy kinda staring at me from across the street, just a random guy getting off the bus, and I thought it was my brother. He was waving to me. Like he was saying goodbye, Max. Sometimes our eyes, our minds—our *hearts*, Max—play tricks on us. You manifest them, but they're not really real.

    Beat.

MAX   Hatch, your brother's still alive.

    Beat.

HATCH   Shit, maybe that was him. The point, Max... is *closure*. Y'know, you're dealing with this whole heart-attack thing; you get all spooked, conjure up your dead wife... you see where I'm going with this? Besides, you've got the whole CCNC negotiation going on, Chinese people everywhere (I mean, more than usual) it's shorting a few wires up there. Stress, my friend. You lose your hair, your... teeth, maybe... but you can't lose *perspective*, Max.

    Beat. MAX is buying it.

MAX   You're right, you're... probably right... I'm just tired. Drunk. I've lost a lot of blood.

HATCH   Attaboy, killer. Okay—oh!—on the topic of—not to aggravate the—but the Chinese thing... you can relax. It's over.

MAX   Over? Over how?

HATCH   Upstairs worked it out. Here's the deal: we give 'em *partial* redress at one percent, two at the most, that's sustainable. Nothing for the families, we put that money into education. A blanket statement acknowledging past wrongs, but in no way is it about liability today. Says it right there in the text. We figure that's enough, not really concerned about public awareness anymore. Y'know? I sign the papers on Friday and the whole thing's done like dinner.

MAX   It's done?

HATCH   Thanks to you, cupcake. Good job.

    Beat. MAX is sullen.

Max, this is great news. Negotiation over. Big bonus coming your way. Promotion, probably. And they get what they get. Now c'mon... Is there something? Like a thing?

MAX   What? No. Just feeling—what is that—melancholy, I guess.

HATCH   Melancholy? What are you, a painting?

MAX   It's probably the—the bourbon and the—dreams, I guess. But...

    Beat. HATCH is listening. MAX reluctantly shows him the article again.

This guy, right? He led raids into Chinese homes, businesses, without warrants—that was legal. A rights violation like that... it was legal. But it only applied to the Chinese. They were detained, beaten—killed, some of them...

HATCH   Not our problem...

MAX   That was '43, right? *(He shuffles papers and finds another.)* This one, uh... '51. Okay... this guy, same MO, throat slit... he was a snakehead, y'know? Smuggled people in and— .

HATCH   Again, not our—

MAX   But it is, though. It is because the tax put these guys *into* business. The Exclusion *kept* them in business. *(Beat. He presses his hand into the paper, like he wishes it would sink into the table and be lost.)* Hatch. This one is from 1964...

HATCH   What, Max?

MAX   My father. This is how my father was killed. *(He shows* HATCH *the article.)* It's right there. He was executive secretary of a labour union, you remember that? That union, along with 231 other organizations, were members of the "Asiatic Exclusion League"... using unions to keep jobs away from Asian immigrants.

HATCH   Your father was killed because he was at home during a break in—

MAX   But what if it wasn't—

HATCH   Then what, huh? What are you saying, Max?

MAX   I don't know. Okay? *(He laughs nervously.)* I don't know! *(beat)* What if it was her... and she's coming for me next?

HATCH   You understand how that sounds?

MAX   I know—

HATCH   I don't think you do. You're paranoid, Max, bordering on delusional.

MAX   I'm only paranoid if they're not after me, but they *are*. SHE is!

HATCH   Even if what you're saying is true. Which is... ludicrous at best... you haven't done anything wrong. You have no reason to be afraid. These guys were all just doing their jobs, Max. I suggest you get back to doing yours.

         Beat.

MAX   My father always talked about his job like... well, like it was God's work. Like he was doing the right thing. And now... *(beat)* What if they deserved it, Hatch? What if... we *all*... deserve it?

Silence. HATCH sighs. MAX broods. Finally, HATCH puts his hand on MAX's shoulder.

HATCH   Sympathy, Max. The great destroyer. This is hard on all of us, and of course you're feeling—what?—responsible? But you're not. *We're* not. When I sign those papers on Friday... it'll be with a heavy heart, Max. But... you'll get your bonus, go home to your kid, and I'll... well I'll probably come right back here. Happy ending.

MAX nods his head.

So let's get you a lap dance, huh Pudding Pop? *(He flags down two girls.)* Hey! Over here, my lovelies. *(to MAX)* You like blonds?

MAX   Um—

HATCH   Okay, I'll take her, you can have this one. She's Oriental, it's kinda fitting.

The girls draw closer. The "Oriental" one is SYLVIA. MAX recoils.

MAX   Fuck!

HATCH   Hey, I said a dance, anything else is gonna—

MAX   I know her.

HATCH   You didn't tell me you were a regular.

MAX   I'm not.

SYLVIA smiles. She is wearing her signature red dress and puts on a fake "Oriental" accent.

SYLVIA   I dancing for you, twenty dolla?

HATCH   Yah, twenty dolla, sweetheart. Enjoy, Max.

MAX   *(aside)* The fuck are you doing here?

SYLVIA   Yes, thank you!

> *She dances up on MAX.*

MAX   Please don't kill me. I'm begging you...

SYLVIA   Yes, thank you!

MAX   Stop that!

SYLVIA   Thank you!

MAX   Look, Hatch, thanks for everything, but... I think I should get going.

HATCH   Oh, c'mon, Maxie. We're just getting started.

> *MAX starts to get up but SYLVIA places her heel on his sternum and pushes him back into the chair.*

SYLVIA   *(aside)* Stay for a bit, Maxie.

> *MAX looks at her leg. He sees the knife sheathed there. It is coated in blood.*

MAX   Jesus! Hatch! Look, look! She's got a fucking knife—she's gonna—

> *HATCH cranes his neck to look over. She smiles at him, the knife is gone.*

SYLVIA   Yes, thank you!

HATCH   You're starting to piss me off, Max.

MAX   Sorry—um—I— *(aside, to SYLVIA)* Look! It's over, okay?

SYLVIA   Did you find Tommy, Max?

MAX   No, I found a kid with a radio and some bullshit story.

SYLVIA You didn't talk to him?

MAX Parlour tricks. Nerve gas or something. "Find the white snake"—
what does that mean?

SYLVIA It means you need to keep looking. Keep looking until you find
him.

MAX No. Fuck it—you want to—what?—stab me? Go ahead. Just get
it over with already. These threats, these visitations—You are not
my Marley. Rattle your chains somewhere else. We're through
here.

Beat. Then, to HATCH.

I have to go. My son—he's waiting for me.

He starts to get up.

SYLVIA No, he isn't.

He stops cold.

MAX What did you say?

SYLVIA Danny's not at home.

*Beat. MAX stares at her. SYLVIA tosses a tiny package, wrapped in
gauze, down at his feet.*

MAX What is—?

He unwraps it. It's a human ear. He drops it and jolts back.

What the fuck? What the—fuck you—you bitch, you fucking—
not my son, not Danny, no not Danny not Danny you bitch you
cold fucking no...

He crumples to the ground, clutches the ear.

SYLVIA   Go ahead, Max. Scream into a deaf ear. That's what my people have been doing for eighty years…

MAX   Take *me*… Kill *me*… Cut *me*…

SYLVIA   I sent you to do a job, Max. You don't do it, there's consequences for that.

MAX   You leave him alone, you fucking cunt, or I'll—

> *His hand raises to her and she grabs it, twisting and breaking two of his fingers. He screams in pain but she clamps her hand over his mouth.*

SYLVIA   You want to save Danny, Max?

> *She traces his face with the tip of her knife.*

Find. Tommy. Jade.

> *She lets him go. She takes the ear gingerly from the floor, re-wraps it, and places it in her purse.*

> *She exits. Beat. MAX leaps up, he grabs the bottle of bourbon from the table and runs out of the room.*

Fourteen: Max vs. The Historian

> *Broadview and Gerrard. MAX walks up and down the street, approaching homeless people and passersby. He has a makeshift splint on his hand.*

MAX   Hey—hey—excuse me—hey! I'm looking for—I'm looking— the one-man TV station? Has—God that sounds inane—do you know him?

> *BIFF Chan creeps up behind MAX, following him down the street. He makes hand gestures to invisible cameras to also follow MAX. He is identical to HAPPY but without all the radio business. He is dressed more as a television floor director, with a baseball cap and headset.*

Excuse me! The one-man TV station, I need to find the—I don't know his name. Excuse me, have you—no, I don't want a god-damn nectarine!

MAX turns and BIFF is right in his face.

BIFF   S'up.

MAX   My god, you—

BIFF   What?

MAX   You look just like him.

BIFF   Who?

MAX   Your brother. Happy.

BIFF   Yah, I bet we all look the same to you, don't we, white boy?

MAX   That's not what I—

BIFF   Whatever.

He sucker-punches MAX in the face and starts walking away.

MAX   Wait! Wait! Your brother sent me to you.

BIFF   Oh yeah?

He keeps walking.

MAX   He let me speak with Tommy Jade!

BIFF stops.

I need to speak with him again. I need to know—find out what happened.

BIFF considers this.

BIFF   Come with me.

> *He leads MAX across the street and into the alleyway behind Jilly's strip club.*

The name's Biff. Biff Chan, the one-man TV station.

> *Beat.*

MAX   Sure. Why not.

> *They stand in the alleyway. There are two beat-up leather armchairs facing one wall. They are pointed at a small TV, set into the wall. It lights up. The screen shows BIFF and MAX talking from thirty seconds ago.*

BIFF   There's a thirty-second delay. I don't like it, but the censors insist… just in case you slip a nipple or something.

MAX   What the fuck are you talking about? You need to help me or—

BIFF   Here, let's elucidate. *(He speaks in the walkie-talkie)* Full screen.

> *The entire wall lights up as one giant TV screen.*

That's sick, right? You should see the shit I got on IMAX.

> *He barks orders into the walkie-talkie.*

Camera One, get close on—what's your name?

MAX   Max.

BIFF   Get close on Max's face. Camera Two, I want a wide shot of the both of us. Camera Three, get coverage in the alleyway. Let's get you some makeup, Max.

> *He breaks out a compact and starts putting foundation on MAX's face. MAX pushes him away but he persists. Although there are no visible cameras, we see the footage on the wall.*

MAX   Can I talk to Tommy now? If I do this?

BIFF   'Fraid not, Huckleberry. See, you met my brother. He's in radio. I'm in television. He can let you talk to Tommy Jade. I can't. S'a different kind of medium, you understand.

Camera Three! Get a profile shot of me explaining this to Max.

I'm a historian. Nothing happens in this town without me knowing about it. Think of it like a documentary.

Camera Two, stay wide.

MAX   You don't get it, I *need* to talk to Tommy again.

BIFF   Well, my brother obviously doesn't think so, 'cause he sent you to me. You can't speak to the man... but I can show you what happened to him.

And Camera One, go in for Max's reaction...

MAX tries to absorb all this.

MAX   Look, I—this—she's got my son. Sylvia, does that mean—do you recognize that name? She's got Danny—my boy—and he's scared, I can feel him—she cut off his fucking ear and—he's autistic, he's got needs—special needs—I need to find him, to help him, so you need to help me. Can you do that?

Pause.

Are you listening—

BIFF   Shh. I'm taking a dramatic pause, give it a sec.

Dramatic pause.

And Camera Three! You say she cut off your boy's ear? Camera One!

MAX   She's going to kill him. If I don't help her.

BIFF   Sounds like Sylvia. Did Tommy say anything, when you spoke to him?

MAX   No, just… "find the white snake." He told me to find the white snake. Whatever that means.

BIFF   Camera Three! Hmm… *(He poses.)* and I'm thinking and I'm thinking, and I give a forlorn look at Max—Max, just cheat a bit that way, good—and I'm feeling sorry for Max, but I'm not sure if I should help, there's drama and a pregnant pause… Okay. I'll help you.

> *Beat.*

And *cut!* Max, that was fantastic. That's gonna look great on the trailer, "don't miss next week's episode"—fantastic.

Great work, Camera One; Camera Two, you were a little slow; and Camera Three, I felt I was dropping out of frame a bit, we should look at that—

MAX   Please!

BIFF   Right. Okay, everyone take five. Max, step over here a sec.

> *They move over to the armchairs and MAX takes a seat.*

The white snake. I remember that episode, that was around 1923 or so.

> *He picks up a remote control and punches some numbers. A TV Guide listing comes up.*

Here it is. Tommy vs. The White Snake. Hey, five stars, that was a good one. Okay. Put on these glasses.

> *He hands MAX a pair of 3-D glasses.*

MAX   Now you're just fucking with me.

BIFF   You gotta put on the glasses if you're gonna watch the show.

> *MAX looks at him. Reluctantly, he puts on the glasses.*

Please turn off all cellular devices and refrain from using flash photography.

> *Opening credits play on the screen. The ensuing scene is played out.*

Fifteen: Tommy vs. The White Snake

> *Simultaneously we are in 1923 and 2006.*

> *2006: MAX watches the scene. Whenever he takes his glasses off, everyone but BIFF disappears. BIFF plays the role of TOMMY.*

> *1923: TOMMY is at the door of COOGAN's house.*

> *He knocks at the door. A blond woman, MIRABEL Coogan, answers in a nightgown.*

MIRABEL   Hello?

TOMMY   Coogan. Looking for Coogan.

> *MAX tears off the glasses. BIFF / TOMMY breaks out of the scene.*

MAX   The fuck is this?

BIFF   What? *(beat)* Oh, you're just in awe of my acting ability.

MAX   You're an actor?

BIFF   I'm the one-man TV station, I do it all.

MAX   Seriously?

BIFF   Hey, I did *two seasons* at Stratford!

MAX   *(under his breath)* Yah, who hasn't...

BIFF   Put the fuckin' glasses back on.

     Miffed, MAX *puts the glasses back on. The show resumes.*

MIRABEL   I'm Mrs. Coogan.

TOMMY   No no... *Mr.* Coogan.

MAX   Wait a sec! Hold on.

     He takes the glasses back off, BIFF *breaks away again.*

BIFF   This is really interrupting my process.

MAX   Did you say "Coogan"?

BIFF   I'm sorry, can you not understand my accent? You want subtitles?

MAX   That was my mother's—what is that—maiden name.

BIFF   Heh. Let's check the credits.

     He hits a few buttons.

     Let's see... Mr. Coogan was played by... Daniel Coogan. Daniel—that ring a bell?

MAX   My grandfather's name. He was an immigration official in Toronto in the twenties.

BIFF   You sure you want to keep watching this? You might not like what you see.

     MAX *takes a deep breath. He puts the glasses back on.*

MIRABEL   I'm sorry, he's not home.

TOMMY   He took money. Insurance. Want it back.

MIRABEL He collected some money from you?

TOMMY   He say "insurance," he bring Chor-swan here, now already September, no one come here, I want insurance back. She need, at home, she need for food and—where is Coogan?

MIRABEL Why don't you tell me your name, I'll tell him you called.

TOMMY   Call? Calling me Tommy Jade.

MIRABEL Oh! You're—my girlfriend Mary, she—your boss's wife. Mrs. Weir.

TOMMY   Missus—okay, I know.

MIRABEL She says you have lovely jewellery for sale.

TOMMY   Uh... Jew——ru—

MIRABEL Lovely jade.

TOMMY   Ah. Thank you.

MIRABEL Would you like to come in?

TOMMY   Um... no, thank you.

MIRABEL Please...

TOMMY   Okay.

> *He enters.* MIRABEL's *parlour room is smoky and dark. She has opium burning on a hookah in the centre of the room. She pulls on it deeply.*

MAX   What is that?

> BIFF *sidebars.*

BIFF   Opium.

MAX   Did Tommy sell that, too?

BIFF   What?

He stalks over to MAX *and takes the glasses off him.*

MAX   I'm just saying, the Chinese trafficked opium into Canada, everyone knows that.

BIFF   Oh yeah? Everyone knows that? Where do you grow opium?

MAX   China, I guess.

BIFF   Wrong, India. And who owned India in the nineteenth century?
White people. The British. They grew opium in India and shipped
it via the East India Company, a British trade organization that
existed for the sole purpose of exporting opium to Shanghai
and Canton. They enslaved the Chinese with opium, fought a
war over it, took Hong Kong… and you say the *Chinese* brought
opium to Canada? Who the fuck owned Canada?

MAX   *(muttering)* The British.

BIFF   Watch the goddamn show.

He throws the glasses back at MAX, *who puts them on.*

MIRABEL   Would you like some?

TOMMY   No thank you.

MIRABEL   Have some, it's *really* good.

She is getting higher and higher. TOMMY *is getting a little buzzed
just from being in the room.*

C'mon…

She slips the hose in between his lips. He becomes almost immediately intoxicated.

TOMMY   Not feeling so good…

MIRABEL   Give it a second. Here, lie down.

She lays TOMMY *down on some cushions on the floor. She hovers over him.*

Daniel's not going to be home until next month. He's out. He goes out, you know. Official business and—what is that? Official. Screening you people. Sending your wives and daughters back, those who set sail after we closed the ports. But he doesn't send all of them back. Some of them he keeps. They're exotic. He—he likes that. Official…

She starts undoing TOMMY'*s shirt.*

So maybe I like that too, don't I? Tommy—Tommy Jade. You got a wife, Tommy? Is she lonely without you? I'm lonely, Tommy. I'm very lonely.

TOMMY *tries to resist, but the opium incapacitates him, weakens him, and despite himself, he enjoys it.*

Just lay back, Tommy Jade, this is official business.

She begins to take off her clothes.

BIFF *turns to address* MAX.

BIFF   Now the next part is a little explicit. Viewer discretion is advised. If you don't want to watch, I understand… technically s'your grandmother, after all. But if you could just give me five minutes…

MAX *looks at him in disgust.*

Right, okay, we'll just fast-forward.

He removes himself from the scene and presses a button to fast-forward. The image begins to distort.

Shit. Oh, motherfucker don't—

MAX What's going on?

BIFF Just a—oh!

The screen turns blue.

MAX What the hell is—

BIFF Cable's out.

MAX What? No! Can't you... Do something!

BIFF Sorry, s'outta my hands.

MAX grabs BIFF by his collar and shoves him against the wall.

MAX My—I have a child. His life depends on you—on *us*—and *this*. So you will fix the goddamn cable!

The nose of a .45 pistol pushes up under MAX's chin.

BIFF Bitch, you wanna back up.

MAX relaxes his grip.

MAX Just... relax, okay? I'm... I'm sorry.

BIFF thrusts the gun at MAX's face.

BIFF You want to see the rest, motherfucker?

MAX Please. It's very important.

BIFF Cable's out. Means you gotta go deeper.

MAX   I don't understand.

BIFF   Deeper. Opposite of shallow. You're familiar with shallow.

MAX   Where? How?

BIFF   You gotta go to the archives.

MAX   On Spadina?

BIFF   No, jackass, it's a metaphor.

>   *He cocks the pistol.*

>   You gotta cross to the other side.

MAX   Whoa, hey, hang on… you're going to shoot me? There has to be—I mean—another way.

>   *Beat.*

BIFF   Well… you could sing.

MAX   I'm sorry?

BIFF   Sing. Music, my pale friend, is a transcendental conduit. It is a way to commune with those from across this plane.

MAX   Are you serious?

BIFF   A'ight, option B.

>   *He aims the pistol. MAX starts awkwardly singing "Put a Little Love in Your Heart."*

>   Louder.

>   *He sings louder, stilted and out of tune.*

>   With feeling.

He goes full tilt. BIFF joins in at key lines in the chorus. There is a big finish. MAX is sweating bullets.

Pause.

MAX   Am I——was that okay?

BIFF   Naw, I just wanted to see if you'd do it.

He shoots MAX in the head. MAX disappears.

Sixteen: Sylvia vs. Danny

SYLVIA's den in Chinatown. The barest of essentials: a cot, blanket, small lamp. Incense is burning to keep the smell of mildew and dead things at bay. DANNY is curled on the cot, the blanket haphazardly thrown over him. SYLVIA crouches near him, watching him, slowly smoking a long cigarette. She is throwing playing cards into an old can. DANNY stirs. SYLVIA's eyes dart to him. He starts to moan. She tries to ignore him. He moans louder, rocking back and forth. She is getting annoyed.

SYLVIA   Hey. *(beat)* Hey. *(beat)* Stop that.

He is still moaning, rocking, not even acknowledging SYLVIA. She throws a playing card at him. Without looking, he catches it and puts it down carefully in front of him.

DANNY   Black.

Curious, SYLVIA throws another card, which he catches like the first and lays it down.

Black.

She tosses the deck to him, not at him, but towards him. They scatter a bit but he swipes them up and begins laying them down in separate piles for red and black.

Red. Black. Red. Red. Black. Red...

SYLVIA   You like those, huh?

DANNY   Yes.

SYLVIA   Whatever keeps you quiet.

> *DANNY quietly stacks and restacks the cards for a while.*

DANNY   Is Max coming soon?

> *Beat. She has no intention of answering him.*

SYLVIA   Why do you call him Max?

DANNY   His name is Max.

SYLVIA   But he's your dad. You should call him "Dad."

DANNY   That's not his name. His name is Max.

SYLVIA   You should call him "Dad."

DANNY   Why?

SYLVIA   *(short)* Because I said so.

DANNY   What do you call your dad?

SYLVIA   I... nothing. I don't call him anything.

DANNY   That's worse than calling him Max. *(beat)* What's your dad's name? You can call him that...

SYLVIA   No more questions.

DANNY   When is Max coming?

> *In one quick motion, SYLVIA is upon DANNY, the knife to his throat.*

SYLVIA   No more questions.

DANNY shuts up. SYLVIA withdraws the knife and lights another cigarette.

Seventeen: Sylvia vs. Coogan

MAX wakes up. It is 1924. He is lying outside COOGAN's house. TOMMY is standing over him. MAX blinks. He stares at TOMMY. TOMMY waves.

TOMMY   Hello.

MAX   What—the wha—

TOMMY   Um. *(He points to himself.)* Tommy.

MAX   The—where are— Biff, the fuck is—fucking—what is—

TOMMY   You speak English?

MAX   Oh, this isn't happening, not *fucking* happening—

TOMMY   *(sighs, to himself)* Immigrants…

MAX   Tommy? Tommy Jade?

TOMMY   Hello.

MAX   How did I get here?

TOMMY   I find you. Here. You know Coogan?

MAX   What? Do I—no. Not really. Look, I need you to come with me.

TOMMY   Come where?

MAX   *(at a loss for that answer himself)* Back… to the future? *(He cringes.)*

TOMMY   *(no idea what MAX is talking about)* Okay… later, I go. Busy right now.

Dismissing MAX, he knocks on COOGAN's door. COOGAN answers.

COOGAN Tommy?

TOMMY Jesus.

>   *COOGAN looks at MAX.*

COOGAN Who the hell are you?

MAX Me? I'm... uh... I'm Tommy's... lawyer.

>   *COOGAN looks at TOMMY, a little frightened.*

COOGAN Your lawyer?

TOMMY Okay.

COOGAN *(nervous at MAX's presence)* Come in...

>   *TOMMY continues inside. MAX follows him, then COOGAN. MAX recognizes the parlour instantly, though it's become a mess. Bedsheets and papers are strewn about helter-skelter.*

Sorry about the state of things here. Can I get you a drink?

TOMMY Okay. *(He doesn't get him one.)*

MAX What's going—

COOGAN Our first child. *(grinning)* Baby girl, born just a few days ago.

MAX Ah. Congratu— *(It dawns on him. He looks from TOMMY to COOGAN and back.)* Oh, fuck.

COOGAN What?

MAX Nothing.

>   *Beat.*

TOMMY You have "insurance"?

MAX   Tommy…

COOGAN   Yah, I got insurance.

TOMMY   Can I have? Back?

COOGAN   Oh, that! The insurance for— *(a hesitant look at MAX)* The special favour?

TOMMY   Yes.

COOGAN   Heh. That's a—it's a complicated— *(changing gears, addresses MAX)* You a local? I haven't seen you before…

MAX   I just moved here from… somewhere else.

COOGAN   Junior barrister?

MAX   King's Counsel.

COOGAN   My mistake.

           Beat.

           Hey. Do you two want to see my baby girl? *(He calls upstairs.)* Mirabel! We have company. You two ladies want to join us?

TOMMY   You explain. Please.

COOGAN   We don't have time for a lesson right now, Tommy. Okay? We'll discuss it at a more opportune time. *(to MAX)* You got kids? *(He lights a cigar and gives it to MAX.)*

MAX   A son.

COOGAN   Oh, a son! I would've— *(in confidence)* A boy would have been my choice. Y'know? Carry on the family name and all. But I heard… y'know, if you really want a boy… you have to… do it… in a special way. From behind, like. Or kind of… like a wheelbarrow? I don't even… is that what you did?

Awkward beat.

MAX   Do you have any bourbon?

COOGAN   *(embarrassed)*Yah, uh... sorry... let me get that for you.

> *He pours him a glass of bourbon.* MIRABEL *enters with the baby in her arms. She freezes when she sees* TOMMY. *They stare at each other.* COOGAN *notices she's arrived.*

There she is!

> MIRABEL *smiles uncomfortably at* COOGAN. *She comes further into the room.* COOGAN *rushes her and takes the baby. She flinches when he touches her.*

Let me see my daughter! Mira, this is Tommy, he's a—a former client, he just—and this is his... friend... uh...

MAX   Max.

MIRABEL   I don't feel well, I should go lie down.

COOGAN   *(laughing)* That's all you've been doing for days, Mirabel. *(to the men)* I tell her, there's only one kinda woman that spends her life on her back, and you ain't it, right! *(He laughs more and takes* MIRABEL *by the arm. Her face shows how hard his grip becomes.)* You don't want to be rude to our guests, do you?

MIRABEL   Of course not. *(She looks at* TOMMY.*)* The Oriental... does he have to be here? They have diseases—Chinese leprosy—and the baby...

COOGAN   Mira, don't be unkind. Tommy's a friend. He's welcome here. Tommy, hold the baby.

> COOGAN *tries to put the baby in* TOMMY's *arms but he refuses.*

TOMMY   Sorry. Very nice baby, but need "insurance" back.

MAX   Tommy, he's obviously very busy, we'll come back another time. *(He tries to shove* TOMMY *out the door, but he is immovable.)*

COOGAN   It's okay, Max. *(He winks at him and addresses* TOMMY.*)* That money has already gone to one of our agents who is bringing your wifey here. These things take time, Tommy, you have to understand that. But I give you my word she is on her way to you. I swear on my baby's beautiful heart she is on her way. Here, *(He takes a dollar out of his pocket and presses it into* TOMMY's *hand.)* buy yourself a new hat or something. Look good for that sweet honey of yours. Okay? *(He releases* TOMMY's *hand, who examines the dollar.)*

MIRABEL   He's upsetting the baby.

COOGAN   The baby's fine.

TOMMY   Need all money. Not dollar money. Chor-swan, she not come now. I hear about no-Chinese law.

MAX   The Exclusion Act.

COOGAN   *(shoots a look at* MAX, *then smiles at* TOMMY*)* That's just a... it's a temporary law, Tommy. It's not permanent. Look, I have it on good authority that ban will be lifted in the next... six months.

TOMMY   Want back. Mrs. Coogan know, I come before, you not answer.

MIRABEL   *(an outburst)* Tommy, please leave!

> Beat. She has spoken out of turn and too passionately. COOGAN *eyes them suspiciously.*

COOGAN   You two know each other?

> TOMMY *lowers his eyes but doesn't answer.*

MIRABEL   I forgot. He came by last fall, you were... away. I thought I told you... I'm sorry.

> Beat.

I should put the baby down.

COOGAN   Sit a spell, Mira.

MIRABEL   She's tired...

COOGAN   Max can take her. Max, I want you to hold my daughter.

MAX   I'm not really good with—

The baby is put into his arms.

Okay then. Um... *(He holds the baby awkwardly.)* She's heavy. I forgot how heavy they are.

COOGAN   She's a month premature, but you wouldn't know it. I was away on business until October last year. That's only eight months. What a miracle, huh?

MAX   Yah... miracle. Tommy, I really need to speak to you outside.

TOMMY has perked up.

TOMMY   September.

COOGAN   *October...*

TOMMY   *(looks at MIRABEL, wide-eyed)* September?

COOGAN catches this. He begins to put it all together.

MIRABEL   Tommy, you must leave now.

COOGAN   What is this?

MAX   It's nothing. *(beat)* You've been very kind, but we've bothered you enough. My office... we're going to write Tommy a cheque for the money you owe him and no one's going to bother you anymore. We're just going to walk out that door. Okay? *(to TOMMY)* Tommy? Okay?

Beat.

TOMMY   What is name? For daughter?

COOGAN   Sylvia. After my mother.

MAX   What did you say?

TOMMY   Sylvia.

> *MAX sits down.*

> *(takes a jade necklace from his pocket)* For Sylvia... a gift.

MIRABEL   No.

COOGAN   What's the matter, Mira? You're old friends, aren't you?

> *She is quiet.*

> You should thank him, Mirabel.

MIRABEL   *(quietly)* Thank you.

> *COOGAN takes the baby and hands her to TOMMY.*

COOGAN   Why don't you give it to her? Go ahead.

> *He gives the child to TOMMY. He holds her, and the moment he does it is clear to everyone the child is his. He fixes the necklace around her neck. He hands her back to MIRABEL.*

TOMMY   We go now. Thank you.

COOGAN   Stay.

> *MAX looks up.*

MIRABEL   He wants to go, let him go.

MAX   We have to be somewhere.

COOGAN   You go ahead. Tommy can stay. Look at this baby, eh Tommy? Look at her. *(He stares at SYLVIA.)* Mira said her face would fill out, didn't you, Mira? You said it wouldn't always have that shape. Those eyes. *(beat)* Just look at those eyes.

MIRABEL   Daniel...

   Beat.

COOGAN   My mother, she was a dog breeder. Did I ever tell you that, Tommy?

TOMMY   No.

COOGAN   Oh yah, she was... she was great at it. Malamutes, field spaniels. Fine bird dogs, the spaniels. My mother, she would always make me watch the birthing. "Gift of life," she said.

MAX   Great story, thanks for the drink, Tommy, we gotta—

   COOGAN glares at him. He shuts up.

COOGAN   The problem was always strays getting into the kennel. When the dogs were in heat, these strays would somehow find their way in. Animals, you know. Can't help themselves.

MIRABEL   Please, just give her to me.

   He ignores MIRABEL and puts the baby in the crib.

COOGAN   So when a new litter was born, my mother... she would check them all one by one. Hold them by the scruff of their neck, and she'd look into their eyes. You can always tell a mutt, she said.

   He draws a Colt revolver from his belt, sticks it in the crib and fires. Blood gets on his face.

   TOMMY bolts up. He rushes COOGAN, they fall to the ground. The gun goes off. TOMMY goes limp. COOGAN gets up. MAX rushes to TOMMY, but

he's already dead. COOGAN reaches into the crib and rips the jade
necklace from SYLVIA. He throws it on TOMMY's body and spits on it.

Goddamn animals.

MAX opens his mouth, but before he can say anything, there is a
sound from the crib. The baby is crying. Everyone turns to look.
COOGAN wipes the blood from his face and looks at it. A stunned beat.
MAX stands, picking up the necklace from TOMMY's body.

MAX   "When the flaming lute-thronged angelic door is wide;
When an immortal passion breathes in mortal clay;
Our hearts endure the scourge."[8]

COOGAN pushes the muzzle of his gun against MAX's temple.

Not again...

He shoots MAX in the head. The world goes black.

Eighteen: Max vs. The Deafening Silence

The darkness. A light flickers on. The TV from the alley. It's a blue
screen that says "NO SIGNAL." There is no one there, the alleyway is
completely deserted. MAX looks around.

MAX   Biff?

No answer.

Sylvia?

No answer.

Come on! I did everything you asked me to! Now what? Take the
blue pill? What? *(beat)* You can't just leave me like this!

Beat. No one is answering, MAX becomes discouraged.

---

8   "The Travail of Passion," W.B. Yeats.

I don't even remember where I parked!

He digs through his pockets for his keys and finds COOGAN's revolver in one of them. He holds it, staring incredulously at it.

What is this?

To the heavens.

The fuck am I supposed to do with this?

Beat. No response. MAX ponders the gun. Beat. He fishes out his cellphone and makes a call.

We need to talk.

He walks off.

Nineteen: Sylvia vs. The Queen of Sparts

SYLVIA's den. She is burning Hell money into a pot while DANNY counts cards. She says a little prayer before each bill she burns.

DANNY   What are you doing?

Beat. She considers the question.

SYLVIA   You and Max don't do this? For your mother?

DANNY   Max says I shouldn't play with fire.

SYLVIA   It's not playing. *(beat)* It's for my father. You burn this stuff here and he gets it in Heaven. I'm sending him money so he won't be poor in Heaven. You can send lots of things. Servants. Mansions. *(She nods at his cards.)* Or tiles so they can play mah-jong. *(beat)* When you die, I'll burn those for you so you can have them in Heaven.

DANNY still shuffles the cards, oblivious to SYLVIA's threat.

DANNY   Max bought me cards like these. They were perfect, except there were fifty-two of them. And fifty-two isn't prime, it's not prime. Fifty-three is prime, there should be fifty-three. So Max put an extra card in. But it still didn't help, 'cause now there's one extra red card. So Max, he took the top half of the queen of hearts, and the bottom half of the queen of spades, and he taped them together. So then they were even *and* prime.

> *Beat. Discreetly and carefully, like it was a Fabergé egg, he takes the half-and-half card out of his pocket.*

My half-and-half card. My Queen of Sparts. Half-and-half. Like me. Just like me.

> *Beat.*

SYLVIA   Me too.

DANNY   We're special.

SYLVIA   We're mongrels. Mutts. We're… less.

DANNY   That's not what Max said. *(SYLVIA scoffs.)* Max said no one can call me a mutt. He said *(aping MAX)* "Danny is not—what is that—half anything… *(the impression fades)* Danny is twice blessed." The best of Max and the best of mother. Twice blessed. Like you.

SYLVIA   Max said that?

DANNY   Before the day she left on the red line and didn't come back.

SYLVIA   Your mother?

> *DANNY nods.*

DANNY   Max didn't talk at all after that for exactly 112 hours and 13 minutes. That's 4.67 days. 0.668 weeks. 0.156 months. And then Max was different. Not the same.

> *Beat.*

You don't want to do this.

Beat.

SYLVIA   Play with your cards, Danny.

> *DANNY shuffles the cards one last time and then withdraws the map he drew for MAX from his pocket.*

DANNY   Can I send something? To Max?

SYLVIA   Max isn't dead. Yet.

DANNY   But he needs it.

Beat.

SYLVIA   Fine.

> *DANNY puts the map in the pot. He's about to strike the match when SYLVIA stops him.*

Wait. You say a prayer first.

> *DANNY lowers his head. His lips move. He looks up at SYLVIA.*

Now.

> *He strikes the match and drops it in. The map slowly burns.*

Twenty: Max vs. The Right Thing

> *MAX's living room. Darkness. MAX paces. He smokes and drinks with his one good hand. There is another figure, vaguely lit, sitting in a chair. MAX speaks to him.*

MAX   Thanks for coming. I appreciate that. You've always been—and it's good to have that—to be that, I mean. A friend. I guess.

I can't say I'm… clear on what's happened over the last week. *(beat)* I've had a heart attack. Been shot in the head. Twice. Stabbed in the leg. My hand's broken. My teeth have been pulled out. And if I hadn't been drunk through most of those things I'd probably be a lot worse off than I am now.

But you see, the thing is… I got another hand. I got more teeth. Only one heart, I guess, but the point is… I would have them shoot me, break me, pull me apart piece by piece. Whatever it takes… to get my son back.

They took my son. My—who does that? Who takes a child away from his father? Who holds a family as fucking *ransom*? *(beat)* These are the questions I've been asking myself. Been trying to—understand, right? Negotiating with myself. And you know what I realized? *We* do. *We* do those things. And then we—what—what, we give them a cheque? Say "sorry"? Where's the fairness in that, Hatch? Where's the justice in that?

> *He turns on a lamp and we see* HATCH *is the figure in the chair. His hands are bound behind him and there's duct tape over his mouth.* MAX *removes the tape from* HATCH's *mouth. He gulps in some air.*

HATCH   This is going in your quarterly review.

> MAX *laughs with sincerity.*

MAX   That's funny. That's something that—you know—you would say that.

HATCH   C'mon, Max. I've been on a few benders in my time too. I won't… I'm not going to hold you responsible for this. Just untie me and we'll get you into a program or something. Get you some help.

MAX   But I *am* responsible, Hatch. We're *all* fucking… responsible. I've seen it. With my eyes, I've seen it.

HATCH   I don't know what you're—

MAX   Did you sign the papers yet?

HATCH   What papers, the—what, the Chinese thing? Is this about...

MAX   Did you sign them?

HATCH   It makes no difference. It's done.

MAX   No. No, you said you were the guy. You were the guy who had to sign, if you didn't sign... this can go away. We can make this right again.

     Beat. HATCH *laughs.*

HATCH   Is that what—? You fucking idiot. You think it's that easy? I don't sign that paper, someone else does it. It's *done*, Max.

MAX   No... no, you *said*—

HATCH   I say a lot of things.

     Beat. MAX *deflates.*

     It's a dead issue. No one wants to deal with it anymore. They get what they get, it's all pretty much the same thing. It's done.

MAX   It's not done. It's never done.

HATCH   So this was your big plan? Hold me hostage and... what? Demand more money? Redress for descendants? What?

MAX   It's not about the money.

HATCH   *(laughs)* It's always about the *money*.

MAX   Not this. This is... what is that—the right thing, Hatch. It's about doing the right thing.

HATCH   Spare me the altruism, Max. It doesn't suit you.

MAX   There's gotta be… something, I have to… I'm *supposed* to do
            something.

HATCH   Lemme tell you something, Max. I hate these fuckers. Okay? Off
            the record, you want the truth? I hate them. And everyone like
            them. They treat Canada like its one big alimony cheque, and
            everyone wants their due. They paid a fucking tax. Jesus, *I* pay
            taxes, I don't ask for it back. Because it's what I owe, Max. I
            owe that to my country. And you know what, buddy? They owed
            it to my country too. We gave them opportunity. We gave them
            work. Wages. And I'm sick and fucking tired of every Tom, Dick
            and Wong crying about how they "suffered." If it's not the Head
            Tax, it's the Exclusion Act. You got the Indians yappin' about the
            residential school bullshit, the Japs and the internment, Blacks
            with their drugs and guns, Raghead-fucking-terrorists turning
            Toronto into fucking Baghdad… But *we're* the bad guys?

            I'm sick of it! Cry cry cry about the goddamn *state* of things.
            But you say this stuff, Max, and people think you're a Nazi.
            White people are the minority, Max. We're giving jobs out to
            coloured people left, right and centre, qualified or not; they can't
            speak English, we let 'em wear their towels on their heads, even
            though—I mean *come on*—you live in *Canada* now; we give them
            all this shit, Max… and *we're* the racists? That's a joke. That's a
            goddamn bumper sticker.

            They come to this country, they take our land, our jobs, our fuck-
            ing *air*… and *Canada* owes *them* something? Suck my big white
            dick, you fucking cunts. You want the truth, the god-honest
            truth, Max? If I had my way, those chink fucks would *still* be pay-
            ing the tax. So fuck them and fuck you. Now get me outta this
            goddamn chair. You're a disgrace to Canada, Max. A fucking dis-
            grace. *(short beat)* Sympathy? *(He spits on the ground.)* There's your
            fucking sympathy.

            *Silence. Fire is coming out of HATCH's eyes. MAX stares at him. He
            withdraws the Colt from his pocket.*

            What the fuck are you doing with that, Max?

MAX   I'm ending this.

HATCH   You're not going to kill me.

MAX   You're right, Hatch. I'm not gonna kill you. Because none of this is real. If I shoot you, you don't die. The part of me that is you... *that* dies. That's why I had a heart attack. Your hate... *our* hate... it squeezed my heart until it didn't work anymore. And now I gotta fix that. I gotta fix it for... I gotta do the right thing. *(He smiles.)* I do this... and I wake up again. I get my son back. I get my life back.

HATCH   *(rapidly, realizing his life is in danger)* No... no, Max, this is real. This is really real. Okay? You're real, I'm real, that gun looks very real. The... the articles you showed me. I looked into it, Max, you're not crazy. It happened. She happened. This woman, this killer of killers... she's real. I can help you find her. We can stop her. Just let me outta this goddamn chair and we can stop her.

MAX   There's no stopping her. There's no stopping either of us.

HATCH   Think about Danny...

MAX   I am thinking about Danny.

        He raises the gun to level it at HATCH's head.

HATCH   Max, please...

MAX   "Mere anarchy is loosed upon the world,
       The blood-dimmed tide is loosed, and everywhere
       The ceremony of innocence is drowned."[9]

HATCH   Max!

        MAX cocks the gun.

MAX   "The best lack all conviction, while the worst

---

9   "The Second Coming," W.B. Yeats.

Are full of passionate intensity."[10]

A sound from above. DANNY's map falls from the sky. It lands between MAX and HATCH. There is smoke coming off of it. The men both stare at it.

HATCH   Well that was unexpected.

MAX picks up the map. He opens it. Stares at it, trying to make sense of it.

MAX   Follow the yellow line.

MAX drops the gun. It clatters to the floor.

I was wrong...

MAX moves behind HATCH and starts untying him.

I made a mistake. I thought—but I was wrong.

HATCH is free. He rubs his wrists. He looks up at MAX. Beat.

HATCH   You were going to kill me. Really kill me. Like, for real.

MAX   Sorry about that. You have to understand, I thought—but there's still time. We can still do the right thing, you and me.

He turns his back to HATCH, who staggers over to the fallen pistol.

We were on the red line, but we were wrong. I was wrong. We need to get on the yellow line. You can do it, we can *both* do it. If you'd seen the things I've seen, you'd understand—just look at the map...

He turns around. HATCH is pointing the gun at him.

Hatch?

---

10   "The Second Coming," W.B. Yeats.

HATCH shoots MAX through the heart. It takes a second for MAX to register what's happened. He falls to his knees. HATCH throws the gun down. He looks at MAX; anger, disappointment, betrayal... he walks out the door. MAX is left alone.

Beat.

He dies.

Twenty-One: Max vs. The Yellow Line

2006. The Department of Justice. MAX's office. MAX is face down on his desk in a puddle of bourbon. It is an exact recreation of the moment before he met SYLVIA the first time. SYLVIA enters as MAX wakes up.

SYLVIA   Max.

MAX   What...?

SYLVIA   Are you all right, Mr. Lochran?

MAX   What? I'm... yes, I'm fine. Everything is— *(He fully wakes up with a start. He checks his shirt for a bullet hole. Doesn't find one. He squints at SYLVIA.)* You. *(beat)* Danny, where's Danny?

SYLVIA   Soon, Max.

MAX   Where am I?

SYLVIA   You're at the foot of the rabbit hole.

MAX   Am I dead?

SYLVIA   *(smiles)* "What's dying but a second wind?"[11]

           Beat.

MAX   So all that was what—a dream? That's a little *Dallas*, isn't it?

---

11   "Tom O'Roughley," W.B. Yeats.

SYLVIA   Maybe. Maybe a dream brought on by too much stress and bourbon. Or maybe just a story you heard once and couldn't forget.
Does it matter?

Beat. MAX searches his pockets.

MAX   I need a cigarette.

*He retrieves a packet of cigarettes and reaches in, but pulls out the
jade necklace he took off TOMMY's body. Beat. He looks at SYLVIA. A
moment. He holds it out to her.*

Tommy wanted you to have this.

*SYLVIA reaches out and takes the necklace from him. She presses it
against her heart.*

Beat.

Look. I'm sorry as hell for what happened to you. But… what
if Hatch was right? All this for… they're gonna get what they're
gonna get.

SYLVIA   It's not the destination. It's not even the journey. But the strug-
gle, Max… now *there's* a *thing*.

She rests her hand on the door, about to leave.

Wake up, Max.

*She is gone. MAX stares at the place she used to be. Beat. He coughs.
Something in his mouth. He spits it out on the desk and holds it up.
His tooth. He grabs the phone on his desk and dials his secretary.*

MAX   Secretary. Is Danny still…? Send him in. Right now, send him—
and hold my calls.

*He hangs up. A second later, the door opens and DANNY walks in,
map in hand.*

DANNY   Hi, Max.

MAX   Danny...

> *DANNY sits on the floor and keeps working on the map.*

DANNY   I'm almost done, Max. To scale and everything.

MAX   Hey... hey, kiddo, it's okay, you don't—

> *SECRETARY buzzes in through the phone.*

SECRETARY
> Mr. Lochran?

MAX   What? I told you I—

SECRETARY
> I know, Mr. Lochran, but you have Thomas Hatch on line one, he
> says it's urgent.

MAX   Can you just—

SECRETARY
> And you have Linda from the CCNC on line two, she also says it's
> urgent.

> *MAX looks at DANNY.*

MAX   Danny, I—

DANNY   *(without looking up)* It's okay.

> *Beat.*

SECRETARY
> Mr. Lochran?

MAX   I... just gimme a...

DANNY   Dad.

  Beat. They look at each other for a moment.

 It's okay.

  Beat.

SECRETARY

 Mr. Lochran? Line one or line two?

  MAX goes to his phone. He slips on his earpiece. He takes a deep breath. He presses a line. He opens his mouth.

  Blackout.

  End of play.

Acknowledgements

I loathe sentiment, but I do owe a tremendous debt to the people who championed this play. They were, in the end, louder than those who tried to shout it down. That in mind, my thanks to Nina Lee Aquino; Guillermo Verdecchia; Yvette Nolan; Don Hannah; Jean Yoon; Philip Adams; Richard Zeppieri; Leon Aureus; Ron White; Richard Lee; Paul Lee; Layne Coleman; Matt White; fu-GEN Theatre Company; the original cast and creative team, whose creativity and generosity were instrumental to the play's final evolution; and to Anita Majumdar, for not killing me in my sleep during the process when many wouldn't have thought twice, if at all.

David Yee was born and raised in Toronto. He is Hapa, of Scottish and Chinese descent. In addition to being a playwright, Yee is an actor and Artistic Director of fu-GEN Asian Canadian Theatre Company.